Cambridge Elements ☰

Elements in Reinventing Capitalism
edited by
Arie Y. Lewin
Duke University
Till Talaulicar
University of Erfurt

STATE-OWNED ENTERPRISES AS INSTITUTIONAL ACTORS IN CONTEMPORARY CAPITALISM AND BEYOND

Olivier Butzbach
University of Campania "Luigi Vanvitelli"

Douglas B. Fuller
Copenhagen Business School

Gerhard Schnyder
Loughborough University

Luda Svystunova
Loughborough University

Shaftesbury Road, Cambridge CB2 8EA, United Kingdom

One Liberty Plaza, 20th Floor, New York, NY 10006, USA

477 Williamstown Road, Port Melbourne, VIC 3207, Australia

314–321, 3rd Floor, Plot 3, Splendor Forum, Jasola District Centre,
New Delhi – 110025, India

103 Penang Road, #05–06/07, Visioncrest Commercial, Singapore 238467

Cambridge University Press is part of Cambridge University Press & Assessment,
a department of the University of Cambridge.

We share the University's mission to contribute to society through the pursuit
of education, learning and research at the highest international levels of excellence.

www.cambridge.org
Information on this title: www.cambridge.org/9781009474108

DOI: 10.1017/9781009474115

First published 2025

A catalogue record for this publication is available from the British Library

ISBN 978-1-009-47410-8 Hardback
ISBN 978-1-009-47412-2 Paperback
ISSN 2634-8950 (online)
ISSN 2634-8942 (print)

State-Owned Enterprises as Institutional Actors in Contemporary Capitalism and Beyond

Elements in Reinventing Capitalism

DOI: 10.1017/9781009474115
First published online: January 2025

Olivier Butzbach
University of Campania "Luigi Vanvitelli"

Douglas B. Fuller
Copenhagen Business School

Gerhard Schnyder
Loughborough University

Luda Svystunova
Loughborough University

Author for correspondence: Olivier Butzbach,
olivierkarl.butzbach@unicampania.it

Abstract: This Element qualifies the common understanding of state-owned enterprises (SOEs) as mere instruments of the state and instead conceives of them as economic actors in their own right. Specifically, SOE top management teams have leeway to diverge from goals that the state they are owned by pursues. Through "institutional work" they can even actively shape the institutional framework in which they are embedded. However, the extent of SOE top management teams' leeway for agency is determined by macro- (country), meso- (state–SOE governance system), and industry-level factors. These factors, in turn, vary from country to country and over time. In other words, SOE agency is "embedded agency." Combining institutional work and historical institutionalist analytic lenses, this Element presents a multilevel model for understanding the embedded agency of the top management teams of SOEs in contemporary capitalism. The model adds an important element to our understanding of the "new state capitalism."

Keywords: state-owned enterprises, state capitalism, embedded agency, institutional work, top management teams

ISBNs: 9781009474108 (HB), 9781009474122 (PB), 9781009474115 (OC)
ISSNs: 2634-8950 (online), 2634-8942 (print)

Contents

Introduction   1

1 A Multilevel Institutional Work Perspective
  on SOE Agency   7

2 The Macro Environment   28

3 The State–SOE Governance System   34

4 Industry Characteristics   48

5 Combining Determinants: An Overall Framework
  to Account for SOEs' Institutional Work   52

  Conclusion   56

  References   65

Introduction

Capitalism has reinvented itself once again in the wake of the global financial crisis of 2007 and in the following two decades or so. This last reinvention has taken the form of what early twenty-first-century scholars and observers have called the "return of state capitalism" – especially in the context of emerging economies (Alami & Dixon, 2020; Bremmer, 2008; Economist, 2012; Grossman et al., 2023; Musacchio & Lazzarini, 2014; Musacchio et al., 2015; Wright et al., 2021). This trend has brought a renewed interest in state-owned enterprises (SOEs),[1] which are a central element of state capitalism (Kurlantzick, 2016). During the post–World War II era, SOEs were used as agents of public policies in a broad range of countries – from Soviet economies to Western planned capitalist economies such as Italy and France (see, for France, Loriaux, 1999; for Italy, Barca, 1997). Such economic policies were premised on the simple ideas that important resources and services – such as coal, steel, and telecommunications – should be controlled by the state (see Giannetti, 2013) and that corporate and industrial planning would be best performed under the umbrella of the state (O'Hara, 2013). The decades since the 1980s then saw a turn against SOEs and state involvement in the economy – accelerated by the fall of Soviet Communism in the early 1990s – which led to a vast trend toward privatization of SOEs in most of these countries, across many sectors, for a number of decades.

However, the corporate governance scandals of the early twenty-first century in the US (Enron in particular) and the global financial crisis of 2007–2008, together with the assertive use of state tools in relatively successful catch-up development strategies in several large emerging economies – in China, Brazil, Turkey, and India in particular – in the late twentieth and early twenty-first centuries have shaken the confident belief in market forces and private companies' ability to provide economic growth and prosperity for citizens. This has led to a timid rediscovery of industrial policy and state ownership as legitimate state strategies to promote growth and structural change in the economy. This rediscovery has appeared particularly topical in view of low growth rates in many Western countries and the urgent need for a green economic transition. In this context even very economically liberal countries or groups of countries like the EU, the US, and the UK have recently turned toward more state-interventionist

---

[1] We define SOEs as commercial enterprises that are part of the state bureaucracy and that are legally independent entities, but whose shares are to a significant degree owned by the state or its agencies. Ownership stakes can range from full ownership to minority stakes held by the state (Musacchio et al., 2015). Our definition of SOEs does not cover companies that are influenced or controlled by the state through means other than ownership – for example, through preferential loans or regulation and governance mechanisms like "golden shares" (Fuller, 2016; Musacchio et al., 2015), although, as we point out later, non-ownership ties clearly matter for SOEs.

economic policies, including industrial policy and state ownership, often through sovereign wealth fund investments.

While the instruments of state intervention in the economy may look familiar and similar to those of the socialist and planned capitalism past, a closer look reveals that the new state capitalism is very different – most importantly, while the attitude toward the role of the state in the economy may have changed, this change is not generally accompanied by a return to socialist ideology or economic theories. Rather, the new state capitalism is adopted across a broad variety of economic regimes, from (nominally) socialist countries like China to liberal economies that continue to very largely defend capitalist and pro-market discourses. This has led in most cases to a less resolute and at times somewhat reluctant use of the traditional instruments of state capitalism by the latter, but also to a more pragmatic mixing of market and state in more resolutely interventionist and at times less democratic states (see, e.g., Cuervo-Cazurra et al., 2014). Under what one may call "old state capitalism" of the socialist and planned capitalist type (compare with Sperber, 2019), SOEs were often viewed as instruments of the state, established and used to carry out public policy goals like innovation (Bernier, 2017; Tonurist & Karo, 2016), social and political cohesion, and stimulating economic growth and development (Thynne, 2011). Implicitly or explicitly, SOEs were considered to lack autonomy, existing simply to implement government mandates. In other words, observers assumed that governments had far-reaching control over SOEs, the latter being seen as "extensions of public bureaucracy" (Musacchio & Lazzarini, 2014: 2). This was often literally the case in terms of their legal status as branches of the state rather than legally independent firms.

Some authors pointed out early on that this instrumental view of SOEs may be too limited and that SOE managers may have "managerial discretion" and hence agentic autonomy (Aharoni, 1981, 1982). This insight seems all the more important regarding today's state capitalism. "Leviathan 2.0," as Musacchio and Lazzarini (2014) call it, is characterized by different mechanisms through which the state exercises its influence over the economy. In particular, state ownership in general should not be equated with the kind of traditional full state ownership that is managed by central ministries. In many cases, the state is a majority shareholder, but not the only one. There are also cases where the state is a minority shareholder – which implies new types of state–SOEs relations (Musacchio & Lazzarini, 2014).

Non-ownership ties matter, too – even when only supplementing state ownership. For instance, in their work on Polish SOEs Bałtowski and Kozarzewski cite, as instances of non-ownership ties, the Polish state's "golden share" – that is, veto right over important decisions – in some SOEs, its "dominant shareholder position" in others, and the statutory voting caps imposed on certain SOEs (Bałtowski & Kozarzewski, 2016). This is true beyond national varieties of state capitalism (Musacchio et al., 2015) and regardless of the multiple conceptual and theoretical questions raised by the notion of state capitalism (Alami, 2023; Alami & Dixon, 2024; Alami et al., 2022).

The new state capitalism has important consequences for the agentic autonomy of SOEs. There is a growing body of evidence suggesting that, despite being more strongly embedded in state-created institutions than most private firms, SOEs have agency and do not just passively respond to state dictates.[2] They are not mere instruments of the state, but rather actors in their own right.

Actually, prior work had already established that even in contexts where the state plays a very dominant role and where SOEs are fully state-owned – for instance, in state socialist Europe before 1989 and in China prior to 1978 – SOE managers had leeway to pursue their own goals (Stark & Bruszt, 2001). In post–World War II Europe, too, conflicts between government ministries and the SOEs' top management teams existed. Later studies on SOEs in the context of post-socialist transition also emphasize the existence of spaces of agentic autonomy for SOEs in which they can pursue their own strategies (Markus, 2008; McDermott, 2004, 2007). Thus, SOEs may benefit from some degree of structural (budgetary, financial, legal) autonomy that empowers SOE managers, especially in their relationships with the state shareholder (Hafsi et al., 1987; Vernon, 1984). This may lead to an "impunity effect" whereby SOEs are afforded more leeway than privately owned companies to disregard or ignore laws and regulations, despite being part of the state bureaucracy in a wider sense (Cuervo-Cazurra et al., 2014).

This hints at the importance of conceiving of SOEs not as homogenous actors that passively submit to the state's mandate but as composite economic actors in their own right. Upper echelon theory (Hambrick & Mason, 1984) suggests that the role of top management teams is particularly important to understand the agency of organizations. Those top management teams can be of various kinds depending on their composition and how their members were appointed.[3] In the traditional state socialist systems, SOE top management teams were typically appointed through communist nomenklatura processes. In (semi-)democractic settings, top management teams are appointed on the basis of partisanship, electoral cycles, or relationships to governing elites (including royal families and party loyalties). Still other top management teams are appointed through technocratic and meritocratic procedures. Importantly, these different appointment procedures imply different

---

[2] See Butzbach et al., 2022, which lays the foundations for this Element's arguments.
[3] Thanks to an anonymous reviewer for pointing that out.

types of incentives and ties between SOE top management teams and state actors, which will have important consequences for SOE agency (see Section 3).

Scholarly work suggests that the agentic autonomy of SOE top management teams has increased further under the new state capitalism. Most importantly, while traditional SOEs were often firmly and unquestionably part of the state bureaucracy, modern SOEs are characterized by a porous and transient state ownership, where increases and decreases in state ownership share are frequent (Peng et al., 2016) and where a broad range of types of state ownership, from full ownership to majority or minority share ownership, exists (Musacchio & Lazzarini, 2014). In many cases, the state is not the only shareholder in SOEs (Rodrigues & Dieleman, 2018). Here, minority shareholders may wield considerable influence over SOE decisions, especially if the SOE is stock-market listed (Musacchio et al., 2015). The increasingly complex and varied ownership structures of SOEs are loosening the state's grip on SOEs and giving SOE managers more leeway than the classical "SOEs as a tool" view would predict (Markus, 2008, 2012; Stark & Vedres, 2012).

Different states also use different organizational vehicles and governance mechanisms to manage state-owned assets. State ownership can be directly exercised by ministries, or the state can set up an investment fund or resort to a public pension fund to exercise its ownership and control rights over SOEs (Okhmatovskiy, 2010). Such variation in ownership, control, and governance mechanisms opens up a larger space for strategic autonomy for SOE top management teams. Because multiple state actors may formally be responsible for monitoring SOE managers, issues of free-riding on the monitoring efforts of others may arise and/or SOE managers may be able to play off one state actor against another (Apriliyanti et al., 2024; Estrin & Gregorič, 2022; Lazzarini et al., 2021; Musacchio & Pineda Ayerbe, 2018). Overall, the more complex and variegated ownership and governance relationships between states and modern SOEs are opening up spaces in which SOE top management team agency can thrive.

Another reason why more agentic autonomy might be presently attributed to SOEs than in the past concerns the multiplicity of goals that SOEs may be led to pursue, from the public policy goals that may be imposed by the state shareholder – which may be numerous and varied (Vernon, 1984) – to the commercial goals required for the financial and operational sustainability of the SOEs' business – which may be different from what the state shareholder wants. Although such multiplicity of goals was considered in past studies of SOEs (Heath & Norman, 2004), especially in cases of "mixed ownership" (Brooks, 1987), the ubiquity of partial state ownership SOEs in the new state capitalism reinforces the effect that such multiple "bottom lines" may have on SOEs' agentic autonomy. Moreover, in the current context of multiple crises (environmental, political, social), SOEs are even more called upon to simultaneously pursue commercial, social, political, and environmental goals (Adebayo & Ackers, 2022; Musacchio et al., 2015; Teng et al., 2018). Moreover, agency theorists claim that SOEs are subject to lax monitoring (Heath & Norman, 2004; Shleifer & Vishny, 1998) and soft budget constraints, whereby SOEs do not face the same pressures to achieve profitability and efficiency as private firms, because the risk of bankruptcy is eliminated due to the possibility of state bailouts (Kornai et al., 2003). This further enhances SOE managers' leeway to act and decide autonomously from state shareholders.

Nowhere is SOEs' agentic autonomy more evident than in the case of state-owned multinational corporations (SOMNCs). In some cases the internationalization of SOEs is the result of the state pushing SOEs to internationalize as part of a developmentalist or geopolitical strategy (Bass & Chakrabarty, 2014; Finchelstein, 2017; Mariotti & Marzano, 2019). In such situations, internationalization reduces, rather than increases, SOE agentic autonomy, as the state can be expected to try to closely monitor SOMNCs' activities' alignment with state goals. However, when SOEs internationalize in pursuit of commercial or strategic goals set by the top management team rather than being pushed by state authorities, their top management teams can build alliances with stakeholders other than their state shareholder (Choudhury & Khanna, 2014), sometimes other states (Fernandez et al., 2023); SOMNCs can even become co-owned by foreign MNCs (Mariotti & Marzano, 2020). This allows SOE top management teams to mitigate or escape the grip of the domestic state shareholder. This "power escape" can explain why many SOEs have become SOMNCs (Cuervo-Cazurra et al., 2014).

Managerial autonomy in SOEs has traditionally been viewed negatively as a source of inefficiencies (Galal & Shirley, 1995) or corruption (Shleifer & Vishny, 1998). More recent studies, however, have shown that under certain circumstances SOE management autonomy can lead to positive outcomes, such as enhanced innovation activity (Lazzarini et al., 2021). However, a realistic conceptualization of SOEs' agentic autonomy should not only focus on their ability to freely pursue business or commercial strategies; it should also capture another important and often neglected aspect of SOEs in an increasingly politicized world, namely, what scholars call SOEs' nonmarket strategies. These are strategies – such as political lobbying or social projects – that companies adopt to manage their political and institutional environment beyond the marketplace (Mellahi et al., 2016). Academics have recently started to turn their attention toward this aspect of SOE agency, conceiving of SOE managers as institutional actors that have to deal with different, often conflicting pressures and expectations stemming from different institutional settings (Guo et al., 2017; Jing & McDermott, 2013; Raynard et al., 2020; Voinea & van Kranenburg, 2018).

This Element extends the conversation about the return of the state as an economic actor by investigating the factors that determine SOEs' leeway to change, maintain, or create the institutions (i.e., the rules of the game) under which they have to act – an activity that organization theorists call institutional work (Lawrence et al., 2009). In other words, we emphasize here the nature of SOE top management teams as institutional actors. Our premise, drawing on the above discussion, is that SOE top managers are not mere agents of the state; rather, they actively participate in strategies aimed at either changing or maintaining the institutional environment in which they operate. Given the political implications of state ownership, we argue that SOEs' top managers may play a particularly prominent – but largely neglected – role in influencing the country's institutional environment and thus the context for doing business.

We refer to the academic literature on "institutional work" – defined as any purposeful action aimed at maintaining or altering an SOE's institutional environment – to capture this aspect of SOE agency (compare with Lawrence & Suddaby, 2006; Lawrence et al., 2009, 2011; McGaughey et al., 2016).[4] Institutional work provides a way out of the "paradox of embedded agency" (Holm, 1995; Seo & Creed, 2002) that Holm (1995: 398) summarizes in the following way: "How can actors change institutions if their actions, intentions, and rationality are all conditioned by the very institutions they wish to change?" Institutional work provides an answer to that question. In the context of the new state capitalism, institutional work undertaken by SOE top management teams can range from Taiwan's Taiwan Semiconductor Manufacturing Corporation (TSMC) maintaining the Taiwanese state's industrial policy institutional focus on the TSMC itself rather than other segments of the semiconductor industry, to SOEs trying to change institutions, such as EDF lobbying in Brussels *against* the French government's position on clean energy regulations. One bold SOE top manager, David Maxwell of Fannie Mae, pushed the state to create whole new – and ultimately very risky – institutions to finance mortgage lending. The impact that these actions ultimately had on the world's financial system – as revealed during the global financial crisis – illustrates just how important SOE institutional work may be.

---

[4] It is important to point out that in this Element we do not assess whether SOE institutional work is positive or negative developmentally, as the outcomes of SOE institutional work are beyond the scope of our framework. We simply argue here that, through institutional work, top management teams can pursue institutional change, maintenance, or creation. Whether such change, maintenance, or creation is good or bad depends on one's metrics and time frame.

Given the importance of such SOE actions, we seek to answer this overarching research question: What factors determine SOE top management teams' resources, scope, and motivations to defy the state's grip on their SOE and pursue institutional work? We conceive of SOEs as boundedly rational purposive actors whose motives and capability to act are shaped by the institutional setting in which they are embedded. This is a key premise of the historical institutionalist theorizing on institutional change in political science (Mahoney & Thelen, 2010; Pierson, 2004; Thelen, 2004). Indeed, from that perspective, even institutional maintenance requires purposeful action.

Combining the institutional work and historical institutionalist literatures allows us to develop a comprehensive theoretical framework to understand the phenomenon of SOE top management teams' embedded agency. Institutional work provides a more micro-level perspective, which we complement with a more macro-level historical institutionalist perspective that provides a political economic conceptualization of institutional dynamics and compensates for the limitations of institutional work. We thus acknowledge the importance of political factors in SOEs' institutional environment. We contribute simultaneously to the understanding of SOEs' agency and to the theory of institutional change in the institutional work and historical institutionalist literatures.

This Element is organized as follows: Section 1 will present and discuss our analytical framework and the way we use institutional work to overcome the paradox of embedded agency in SOEs. Sections 2, 3, and 4 will examine the various factors that determine the likelihood of the undertaking of institutional work by SOEs' management. In particular, Section 2 will analyze how the state's financial policies, including financial repression, and industrial policies orientation toward SOEs shapes the resources, motivations, and goals of the SOE top management teams to engage in institutional work to shape the state capitalist systems they are embedded in; Section 3 will focus on the "meso" level, that is, the state-governance system; and Section 4 will focus on the ways industry-level characteristics shape SOEs' embedded agency. Section 5 combines all levels to propose a general understanding of SOEs' institutional work. The Conclusion contains with a discussion of the broader implications of our argument, for both the (in)stability of contemporary capitalism and the future trajectories of the "new state capitalism."

1 A Multilevel Institutional Work Perspective on SOE Agency

As discussed in the introduction, a growing stream of empirical research shows that, contrary to still widespread views about them, SOEs are not mere tools of the state. Rather, they often actively engage in autonomous actions aimed at maintaining or transforming the environment they are embedded in. This concerns not only their competitive position in the marketplace but also their embedding in normative societal and state-made regulatory and legal frameworks, which scholars refer to as institutional environment. Institutions – broadly defined as the "rules of the game," both formal and informal (Hodgson, 2006) – put pressure on organizations and individuals to adapt to what is legally binding, societally expected, or more generally considered "the right thing to do" or the appropriate way to behave (DiMaggio & Powell, 1983). However, institutions also provide organizations with resources and capabilities that enable certain strategies and practices – such as high-quality production relying on highly skilled workers whose skills in turn are a result of the institutional system – that would not be possible without institutional support (Jackson & Deeg, 2008).

Institutions vary across capitalist economies (Hall & Soskice, 2001) as well as within different varieties of state capitalisms (Musacchio et al., 2015; Wright et al., 2021). The way in which SOEs and their top management teams seek to influence the institutional environment they are embedded in – in other words, to perform institutional work – can hence be expected to vary as well. The goal of this Element is precisely to identify – based on the organization theory and historical institutionalist literatures – which factors allow us to understand how and when SOE institutional work varies.

Institutional pressures and support for SOEs exist at different levels – the country level, the sector level, the level of SOE governance, among others. We discuss institutional factors influencing SOE leeway for agentic work at all of these levels to develop a multilevel understanding of SOE agency under the emerging new form of state capitalism.

1.1 From SOEs' Agentic Autonomy to Institutional Work

While SOEs are closely tied to their state-made institutional environment – composed of formal rules and regulations, but also informal norms pertaining to the appropriate role of SOEs in the economy – they potentially also have the motivations and resources to actively try and shape that environment in order to enhance their strategic leeway and/or their top management teams' own interests and preferences. Academics have proposed the concept of institutional work to better understand this "paradox of embedded agency" (Seo & Creed, 2002).

As mentioned in the Introduction, institutional work captures the purposive actions of individuals and organizations geared toward establishing, maintaining, or changing institutions. Institutions, in turn, may usefully be defined as the "(more or less) enduring elements of social life that affect the behavior and beliefs of individuals and collective actors by providing templates for action, cognition, and emotion, nonconformity with which is associated with some kind of costs" (Lawrence et al., 2011: 53).

In this Element we argue that understanding how SOEs interact with and try to influence the institutional environment they are embedded in requires a nuanced conceptualization of how and why SOEs act. Institutional work provides such a conceptualization by offering a way of understanding SOE agentic autonomy that shows how individual and collective actors interact with the institutional environment they are embedded in. Firstly, institutional work recognizes that institution building is often the result of cumulative and quotidian behaviors by actors who are embedded in the institutional setting (Lawrence et al., 2011). Unlike the often "path-breaking" nature of change and a focus on changing formal institutions through more specific corporate political activities such as lobbying (Mellahi et al., 2016; Mizruchi, 1992), institutional work encompasses actions outside of formal channels of influence (Lawrence et al., 2009). Secondly, institutional work acknowledges that actions aimed at transforming the institutional environment do not necessarily have to lead to radical change, but can trigger incremental institutional change (Liu et al., 2016). Thirdly, while purposive, institutional work can affect institutional change or maintenance indirectly as a result of actions targeted at other goals than institutional maintenance or change. Indeed, the notion of intentionality lies at the core of the institutional work concept (Battilana & D'Aunno, 2009). As such, institutional work conceives of agency as "an ongoing activity whereby actors reflect on and strategically operate within the institutional context where they are embedded" (Lawrence et al., 2011: 55). Here, intentionality consists of a variety of behaviors, ranging from habitual enactment of taken-for-granted schemas, over conscious and strategic future-oriented transformation of existing institutions, to pragmatic responses to environmental forces (Battilana & D'Aunno, 2009; Emirbayer & Mische, 1998). In some of these cases institutions are not the intended object of agency. Rather, actors shape institutions while pursuing other objectives (Smets & Jarzabkowski, 2013).

The concept of institutional work has been usefully applied to analyzing the interactions between actors and the state apparatus. Thus, Micelotta and Washington (2013) used institutional work to explain how Italian legal professionals successfully opposed governmental reform attempts that would have affected their professional status. Similarly, Yan and colleagues (2018) applied the concept of institutional work to Chinese firms to understand how their interactions with the Chinese state coproduce the institutional context stimulating outward foreign direct investment and thus firm internationalization.

More so than private enterprises, SOEs are considered to be strongly embedded in their institutional environment. This embeddedness may be a source of political constraints on their operations, which is amply explored in the literature on SOEs, especially in relation to economics (see, for instance, Inoué, 2020), but it may also confer political legitimacy on SOEs (Li & Zhang, 2007; Marquis & Qian, 2013). Thus, SOEs' actions can be expected to have political consequences. In many cases they can be expected to be in line with governmental policies and ideology (Hofman et al., 2017). Yet, particularly during periods of "institutional transition" toward a more market- and rules-based – and therefore less state-dominated – institutional order (Peng, 2003), SOEs may see their political influence and legitimacy decline. This may generate incentives for SOEs to challenge policies adopted by pro-market reform governments. Consequently, SOEs may act as a conservative force seeking to maintain the existing institutional order (Micelotta & Washington, 2013). In such situations, SOE top management teams can be expected to leverage political resources to attain their institutional goals of maintaining the status quo.

In yet other cases, SOEs' top management teams may seek to actively change their institutional environment. Specifically, SOEs may use institutional work to reduce the constraints imposed on them by their deep embedding in state-made institutions. This phenomenon has been central in studies on SOE internationalization whose starting point is the view of SOEs as "captives of the state" (Rudy et al., 2016: 76). From this perspective, the key motivation for SOE internationalization is political rather than commercial and associated with goals related to the home country's national interest. Yet, the more recent "power escape" perspective (Clegg et al., 2018; Cuervo-Cazurra et al., 2014; Rodrigues & Dieleman, 2018) indicates that internationalization can allow SOE top management teams to escape the constraints imposed by state ownership by reducing dependence on the government for resources. Internationalization can also constitute the trigger for SOE top management teams to recognize the possibility and desirability of power escape in the first place. Thus, Rodrigues and Dieleman (2018: 40) quote Malaysia's Petronas top management team "as saying they regretted being the government's number one 'piggy bank' as they would rather invest in continued globalization."

To understand when and why SOEs engage in institutional work to try to either maintain or change the institutional constraints they are facing, we need to take into account factors at different levels of a country's institutional environment. These levels constitute both a target of institutional work and its determinant.[5]

---

[5] The notion of "institutional environment" may suggest that institutions are external to the firm. Yet, institutions are often constitutive of SOEs themselves and institutions can be (co-)created through SOEs' organizational strategies (Lawrence & Suddaby, 2006). Therefore, the assumption of exogeneity may be debatable in the case of SOEs even more than in the case of private firms

1.2 The Many Institutional Constraints and Opportunities of SOEs

We unpack in this section the multilevel institutional environment in which SOEs are embedded and differentiate the degree to which each institutional layer is associated with SOE agency. This will allow us to enhance our understanding of when SOEs are more likely to be aligned with state goals and when their top management teams are more likely to pursue their own interests. This may have implications for important economic and societal outcomes, such as the fight against climate change (Grosman et al., 2024).

More precisely, we distinguish three main levels of SOEs' institutional environment: (1) the national institutional level; (2) the regime of state–SOE relations that form the SOEs' governance system, that is, the rules and mechanisms through which the state manages its SOEs (Butzbach et al., 2022) and the governance system that distributes the rights and responsibilities of different actors in and around the SOEs (compare with Aguilera & Jackson, 2003); and (3) sector- or industry-specific institutions. Each of these levels generates a set of resources and constraints that contribute to determining the potential scope of SOE institutional work, while also being, simultaneously, the potential target of SOE institutional work. The extent to which SOEs will be able to perform institutional work and its nature may vary across the different levels affecting the way in which SOEs operate in a given context.

Industry-level rules and regulations are typically the object of strategies summarized under the header of corporate political activity (CPA) (see Lawton et al., 2013), which include well-known strategies of corporations trying to influence political decisions, for example via lobbying or campaign donations, among other things. Such action may include lobbying to maintain entry barriers that favor incumbent firms (Oliver & Holzinger, 2008) or establishing personal relationships with policymakers to reduce regulatory obstacles to SOEs' operations (Guo et al., 2017).

Higher-level institutions, on the other hand, are more difficult to affect through such direct nonmarket strategies, as they potentially affect a wider range of actors beyond any given industry. Coalition-building political strategies – whereby individual firms seek like-minded organizations or other actors who support their cause – may constitute one way in which SOE top

---

(see Battilana & D'Aunno, 2009; Bitektine et al., 2020). The hybridity of SOEs and their "multiple bottom lines" hints at the porosity of the divide between "the state" and non-state entities. Such porosity is also evident in the variety of governance arrangements characterizing state–firm relations. Extant literature suggests that the degrees to which SOEs are exposed to economic or governmental institutional logics (Thornton et al., 2012) may be better conceived of as a continuum rather than a dichotomy (Musacchio et al., 2015; Rodrigues & Dieleman, 2018).

management teams may seek to enhance their influence over such national-level institutions (Oliver & Holzinger, 2008).

Finally, the state–SOE governance system, which most directly affects the relationship between the state and the SOE, may be the most resistant to SOE institutional work, as "state interests" (i.e., the interests of "state actors," broadly construed) are most directly affected by any changes that would favor SOE autonomy.

Countries vary a great deal along each one of these institutional dimensions determining SOE agency. Some of the latter will also vary within any given country, across different sectors, for instance. Therefore, explaining SOE agency in the current context of a return to more state-led industrial policies and ownership requires us to incorporate analysis of potential interactions among SOEs' individual characteristics, their strategic actions, and their institutional environment at multiple levels.

Given the resurgent importance of SOEs in the world economy, such an explanatory framework can help us understand how this trend may affect the evolution of national economies. Specifically, it helps us understand the political factors that underpin institutional change or maintenance, which the academic field of historical institutionalism focuses on (Mahoney & Thelen, 2010; Pierson, 2004; Streeck & Thelen, 2005; Thelen, 2004). Historical institutionalism allows us to capture the dynamic – as opposed to the static or deterministic – ways in which SOEs interact with their institutional environment. It allows us to distinguish SOE top management teams' agency from "actor-centered functionalism" (Pierson, 2004) and structural determinist accounts of institutional stasis that does not allow for any agency (Mahoney & Thelen, 2010; Thelen, 2004). It is such "political dynamics [that] drive institutional genesis, reproduction, and change" (Thelen, 2004: 31). Moreover, political factors partly determine the coalitions that form around specific institutions (Mahoney & Thelen, 2010; Thelen, 2004), which may become a target of SOE top management teams' efforts to change or maintain their institutional environment. Or, in Peter Hall's words, "[a]cknowledging [institutions'] plasticity raises questions about when institutions should be seen as determinants of behavior and when as objects of strategic action themselves" (Hall, 2010: 204).

A key insight of historical institutionalism is that institutional change and maintenance result from similar processes. This suggests that institutional stasis is not merely the result of processes of self-reinforcement and positive feedback – as institutional economists tend to consider – but an outcome that may require institutional adaptation and transformation for these inherited institutions to better fit current political, social, and economic trends (Thelen, 2004: 293). Conversely, institutional change does not automatically "emerge from actors with transformational motives" (Mahoney & Thelen, 2010: 22). Rather, we follow Streeck and Thelen (2005) and Mahoney and Thelen (2010), who have reconceptualized institutional persistence and change as two different modes of institutional change that can be placed on a continuum.

That said, in some respects we diverge from Mahoney and Thelen's (2010) specific theory of institutional change. Thelen and Mahony (2010) theorize the directionality of institutional change on the basis of strong assumptions leading us to view situations of institutional change as struggles over the status quo. Yet, such attempts at theorizing directionality contradict the most fundamental assumptions on which historical institutionalism is otherwise based (e.g., Streeck & Thelen, 2005; see also Zara & Delacour, 2020). In our framework the outcome and directionality of institutional change remain an indeterminate, empirical question.

However, our main divergence from historical institutionalist accounts of institutional change concerns our different analytical focus. Historical institutionalism mostly focuses on processes that cause different types of macro-institutional change. Our framework seeks to zero in more directly on the economic actors involved and thus firm-level aspects of the institution–organization interaction, rather than the macro-institutional framework. Our focus on the *determinants* of SOE top management team agency helps us understand when SOEs are likely to pursue institutional work (and thus institutional change or persistence) or to refrain from doing so. As such, our analytical framework provides a more "upstream" approach to the institutional determinants of SOEs pursuing institutional change or maintenance, while Mahoney and Thelen propose a "downstream" analysis of the "affinity between particular kinds of actors and modes of change" (Mahoney & Thelen, 2010: 27). Before presenting our framework of analysis for SOE agency, we need to spell out the assumptions leading us to focus on SOE top management teams as the key locus of institutional work and our behavioral assumptions regarding both SOE top management teams and state actors.

1.3 Top Management Teams as the Key Locus of SOE Agency

A key assumption on which our framework rests is that SOE agency is tightly associated with SOE top management teams. This assumption is rooted in the long-standing belief that top management is the proper locus of strategic discretion (Williamson, 1963) and the view that organizational behavior reflects top managers' choices, as argued in the "upper echelons" theory (Hambrick, 2007; Hambrick & Mason, 1984). A few decades ago, scholars of SOEs in the business and management literature emphasized how the closeness of SOE top management teams with policymakers encouraged the consolidation of "strategic apex configurations" at the top level of the organization (Hafsi et al., 1987; Vernon, 1984). However, this assumption may appear inconsistent with more recent approaches and studies within other scholarly traditions, notably organization studies in sociology, which see actors at all levels of the organization playing an important role in organizational agency (Edwards et al., 2024). This is especially true for institutional work by SOEs, which may cast doubt on our choice to focus on top management teams. Indeed, like in other organizations, in SOEs, too, actors at all levels may be as politically well-connected to the state apparatus and/or the policymaking authorities as the top management team. This is the case with middle managers in Chinese SOEs who, according to Guo and colleagues, perform a key role in establishing "bridges" with local policymakers and party bureaucrats (Guo et al., 2017). Also, trade unions and their members may be "change actors" performing institutional work in certain contexts (Pandey & Varkkey, 2020). Finally, technical staff may be instrumental in driving changes in regulation concerning health and safety conditions for SOE workers or technical standards for SOE production.[6] In fact, institutional work scholars have been particularly interested in exploring institutional change brought about by actions taken by peripheral actors or, in the context of organizations, low-level employees (compare with Zietsma & Lawrence, 2010).

Yet, in general, SOEs show traits that lend support to our choice to focus on top management teams as the key locus of SOE agency – especially with regard to the kind of institutional work we are interested in. Firstly, the macro-level institutions in which SOEs are embedded, and which may be the target of SOEs' institutional work, are less likely to be affected by the type of boundary work performed by lower-level employees. More generally, strategic decisions with political implications are likely to be carried out by top managers (Rodríguez Bolívar et al., 2015). Again, not all institutional work, even at SOEs, has to do with these kinds of decision or that part of SOEs' institutional environment. This is why we limit our investigation to what we may call "strategically important institutional work," which directly pertains to SOEs' (market and nonmarket) strategies and is therefore bound to be performed primarily by top management teams. Secondly, SOEs are often large organizations that, in many cases, were part of the state bureaucracy at one point in their existence, or at least were closely tied to it by ownership and other political ties. As such, we would expect a certain hierarchical culture to prevail that means that politically

---

[6] This point was helpfully made by participants in a September 2023 workshop at the University Sorbonne Paris Nord, organized by Tristan Auvray, whom we thank here.

sensitive institutional work will primarily be carried out by top management teams, rather than lower levels of the SOE hierarchy. Thirdly, political ties are often skewed toward SOEs' top managers, who are often the direct beneficiaries or carriers of political connections (Betz & Pond, 2023; Wang et al., 2022; Zhang et al., 2023).

1.4 The Multiplicity of SOE Top Management Teams' Goals and Goal Misalignment

Most scholarly works on SOEs and SOE management have explicit or implicit built-in assumptions about behavior that inform their theoretical conclusions. This Element does, too. Our assumption is that action is purposive, but does not have to be rational, self-seeking, or maximizing in a narrow economic sense. Our underlying "model of action" allows for behavior to be driven either by actors striving for satisfaction of material interests or by actors following social norms and values (i.e. informal institutions), which may not be economically rational in a utility-maximizing sense of economic theory. In other words, we assume that human action is multidimensional and therefore use the term *goals* rather than *interests* or *values* when describing the sources of economic actors' motivations. This terminology allows us to describe a desired outcome that a collective or individual actor pursues without making any *a priori* assumptions about the underlying driver of the action in every instance. Here, we do not seek to explain whether top management teams behave in self-seeking ways or are guided by a belief in some public good. Rather, the key question is whether the SOE top management teams' goals – whatever may motivate SOE top management teams – are aligned or not with those of the state and the institutional framework.

In a sense, then, our behavioral assumptions are in agreement with one basic tenet of managerial discretion theory (Williamson, 1963) and agency theory (Jensen & Meckling, 1976), namely, the hypothesis that the goals pursued by business firm managers may differ from and even contrast with the goals pursued by the firm's shareholders. This idea has been applied to SOEs in studies that show that SOE chief executive officers (CEOs) may diverge from what state shareholders demand from them (Apriliyanti et al., 2024). Applied to our context of SOE top management team institutional work, we consider agency conflicts – which we reframe here as goal misalignment – to be a powerful engine behind SOE top management teams' striving for autonomy – and, consequently, behind SOE institutional work.

However, we disagree with another key tenet of agency theory as it is often applied to SOEs, namely, the "grabbing hand" model of the state (Shleifer &

Vishny, 1998; see also Inoué, 2020; Lazzarini et al., 2021).[7] This view argues that SOE managers seek autonomy from state actors because the former's aims to achieve commercial viability/profitability clash with the latter's political goals. We do not reject the possibility that actors controlling state shareholdings do seek to exert control over SOEs to reach political or private goals and may be more or less licit or legitimate (see Apriliyanti et al., 2024). Such a "grabbing hand" was blatantly at work, for instance, in the case of the 2019 scandal surrounding the political use of the Romanian state-owned airline company. The Romanian minister of transportation allegedly ordered the airline's CEO to delay some flights on a particular day in order to disrupt turnout at an important vote on a motion of no confidence against the government (Dragomir et al., 2021). What we contest, however, is the undue generalization of this "grabbing hand" view of the state–SOE relationship, very much informed by a public choice approach to politics and politicians, whereby the latter are *always* driven by political self-interest and SOEs are mere instruments to that end. Indeed, even in the "extended agency framework" used by Lazzarini and colleagues, "politicians" are assumed to be "self-interestedly in pursuit of political divi-dends" (Lazzarini et al., 2021: 564).

An alternative view posits that the state actors may have the public good in mind when establishing SOEs and trying to use them strategically to provide public goods (Aguilera et al., 2021; Bernier, 2017). Yet, here, too, a skeptical view suggests that even if that is the genuine intention of the state, the ability of the state to hold SOE managers to account is limited (Heath & Norman, 2004). This view hence considers managers to be self-interested and motivated by their private goals. This assumption is shared by the extended agency framework, where managerial self-interest extends beyond perks and private benefits of control and includes operational autonomy and career advancement (Lazzarini et al., 2021).

We attenuate these agency-based views in two ways: Firstly, while we posit a certain unity of strategic action on the part of SOE top management teams (see earlier), it is reasonable to assume that state actors may be multiple – that is, the field of state shareholding may be a large field populated by a variety of actors reaching from elected policymakers to ministry of finance bureaucrats to regulators[8] that may seek to pursue a variety of goals as well (see, for the French case, Coutant et al., 2020, 2021; and, more generally, Apriliyanti et al.,

---

[7] One may also point out another important criticism of agency theory, namely, that it unduly conceives of shareholders as principals and managers as agents. See Butzbach (2022) for a summary and discussion of this criticism.

[8] By contrast, the vocabulary used by agency theory scholars often reduces state actors to one category. See the telling example of Inoué (2020), who alternates between calling such actors "politicians" and "state officials."

2024; Estrin & Gregorič, 2022). Secondly, and more importantly, there is no reason to exclude the possibility that state actors or SOE managers are driven by motivations other than self-interest, for example by trust or loyalty (see, e.g., Gintis et al., 2005).

Moreover, the imposition of noncommercial goals on reluctant top management teams by electorally motivated state actors is just one potential configuration of goal (mis)alignment between state actors and SOE top management teams. For instance, a recent study found that minority state shareholdings may be conducive to lower corporate fraud through reduced tunnelling and enhanced internal controls (Zhang et al., 2023); in that case, a "benevolent" state shareholder pursues the viability of the SOE by disciplining managers tempted to pursue private gains instead.

But what are those goals that state actors and SOE managers may likely pursue? The academic literature on SOEs follows two different approaches: The first theoretically derives these goals from existing theories of the firm (Peng et al., 2016); the second deduces them from studies of specific, empirically observed SOE business activities, such as acquiring other firms (Florio et al., 2018), or from historical cases (Cuervo-Cazurra et al., 2014).

We combine these two approaches with other theories of organizational behavior (in particular organizational citizenship behavior and public sector motivation) and identify five overarching categories of goals that SOE top management teams may pursue: economic goals, strategic policy goals, welfare goals, political goals, and private goals (see Table 1). All potential top management teams' goals are goals that state actors may pursue too and they are not mutually exclusive. Rather, any given action undertaken by SOE top management teams may lead to the simultaneous pursuit and attainment of several goals.

"Economic goals" correspond to the economic viability and profitability of SOEs. We distinguish between supra-organizational economic goals when the aim primarily is to generate income for the state and/or to maximize returns for the state shareholder, and organizational (i.e., SOE-level) economic goals, which consist in generating profits and securing firm survival and access to key resources. This distinction is important because there may be goal misalignment or conflicts between state actors and SOE top management teams even when all actors pursue economic goals. For instance, state actors' emphasis on income-generating strategies may clash with SOE top management teams' commitment to the firm's survival. This configuration, we surmise, is actually quite common.

The second category of goals is "strategic policy goals," which correspond to the strategic policy objectives that underpin state ownership in any given SOE – and that may be shared and actively pursued by SOE top management teams as well. State ownership is often justified by the need to address market failures or

Table 1 SOE goals and interests

Category of goals		Illustrations
Economic goals	Supra-organizational economic goals	Generating income for the state Maximizing returns on investment/shareholder value
	SOE-level commercial goals	Accessing key competitive resources, expanding the firm, gaining market shares Ensuring the survival of the firm Generating profits
Strategic policy goals		Promoting economic development Innovation Control of critical strategic infrastructure and resources Support during financial distress Reducing unemployment
Welfare goals		Preventing social unrest Providing essential goods and services
Political goals		Providing rents for key constituencies or politicians
Top management's private goals		Private benefits of control Career advancement

Source: Adapted from Butzbach et al., 2022.

imperfections. In these cases, governments establish SOEs or acquire stakes in companies when they deem that markets or private firms are allocating resources inefficiently (Cuervo-Cazurra et al., 2014). In other cases, state ownership is motivated by the aim to control one particular market segment, industry, or firm, for strategic reasons related to national security, energy self-reliance, international competition for resources, or international competition for innovation in key sectors. This particular motivation has been a constant source of legitimacy for state shareholdings in France (Coutant et al., 2021); it is often associated with industrial policy goals (see Johnstone et al., 2021; Kim & Sumner, 2021).

Strategic policy goals may also be associated with national foreign policy objectives when the SOE operates in sectors such as energy or defense. One may add that the strategic policy goals of state ownership have often, throughout history, been informed by nationalist, socialist, or developmentalist ideologies that consider state control of critical resources to be superior to private ownership. Economic theories – such as import substitution industrialization – that consider state ownership an important tool for national economic development can also lead to strategic policy goals justifying state ownership of firms (Cuervo-Cazurra et al., 2014; Kim & Sumner, 2021).

Goal misalignment may emerge whenever state actors embrace strategic policy goals while SOE top management teams pursue other goals – such as economic ones – and vice versa. Also, goal misalignment may occur as both sets of actors pursue strategic policy goals – when there is disagreement over what those goals should be. One such case was the conflict between the new Norwegian government and state-owned oil giant Statoil in the early 1980s. In 1981, the incoming Conservative government had openly campaigned to curb Statoil's power ("clipping Statoil's wings," its campaign said) and to have the Norwegian state take control over cash flows generated by the oil field jointly operated by Statoil and the state. Eventually, despite a heated political debate and opposition from Statoil's powerful CEO, the Conservatives had their way and the political compromise hashed out in 1984 led to the emergence of a restructured shareholding model and a more powerful state actor compared to Statoil's top management team, a new entity called the "state's direct financial interest" (see Ryggvik, 2015; Thurber & Istad, 2011).[9]

"Welfare goals" is the third category of SOE top management team goals, which refers to the SOE's role in providing public goods, or goods or services, that are not affordable or readily available in the marketplace but are deemed important for the population's well-being. One can cite state-owned utilities

---

[9] See also the official corporate version of the story on Equinor's (formerly Statoil) webpage: https://equinor.industriminne.no/en/curbing-the-cash-flow/ (accessed November 2, 2024).

providing electricity or water, or state-owned transportation companies. More generally, job protection and "minimizing social unrest" are often "legitimate goals" for SOEs (Peng et al., 2016: 299). These goals are sometimes enshrined in law. In Indonesia, Article 33 of the 1945 Constitution states that "Sectors of production which are important for the country and affect the life of the people shall be under the powers of the State." The article is used by some as direct justification for Indonesian SOEs' welfare goals.

The fourth category of SOE goals is "political goals." We narrowly defined them as politicians' (i.e., elected policymakers') *private* interest in conserving power through reelection or regime reproduction in nondemocratic settings. In democracies, such goals generate incentives for politicians to provide rents to their voters (whose support contributes to regime legitimacy and stability), for instance by (over-)investing in certain geographical areas. Thus, SOEs can be very useful tools in this regard. The reason we consider such "political goals" to be among the potential drivers of SOE top management team behavior is that the circumstances may be such that top management teams either fully embrace such goals or have no possibility to eschew the pursuit of such goals as their own.

Of course, the typical goal configuration emphasized in SOE studies drawing on agency theory (and public choice behavioral assumptions) is one where economic goal–driven SOE top management teams seek autonomy from politicians pursuing private goals. However, even in such configuration, managerial autonomy is not the sole desirable objective, from the manager's point of view. In fact, the resource dependency theory predicts that SOEs (and SOE top management teams) will pursue strong political ties with the state bureaucracy in order to secure key resources and to increase "the mutual dependency between these SOEs and officials" (Peng et al., 2016: 309). Similarly, agency theory may also lead us to expect a top management team preference for close ties with politicians if such ties are considered conducive to SOE managers' career advancement.

However, let us emphasize that the goal misalignment between political goal–driven politicians and economic goal–driven managers is just one possible configuration. Politicians may be as interested in public goods, and therefore in making SOEs pursue strategic policy goals or welfare goals, as in their private interest in reelection. Or they may be ideologically committed to non-private goals. Or they may be inclined to view their private interest as strongly tied to the successful pursuit of other goals.

The final category of goals pursued by SOE top management teams is what we call "private goals," which correspond to the behavioral drivers first identified in the managerial discretion literature decades ago, particularly career advancement, on-the-job consumption, perks, high wages, and, more generally, the private benefits of control (Cuervo-Cazurra et al., 2014; Lazzarini et al.,

2021; Musacchio & Lazzarini, 2012; Peng et al., 2016). While these goals exist and may drive SOE top management teams' behavior in many cases, there is no reason why it should *always* be so. Managers may be driven by norm and value orientation, as opposed to material self-interest.

In particular, top managers (like other organizational actors) may attach particular value to the survival and success of their organization – which largely, but not exclusively, falls under the category of "economic goals" identified earlier. This view is supported by the literature on "organizational citizenship behavior," conceptualized by Dennis Organ in 1988 as "individual behavior that is discretionary, not directly or explicitly recognized by the formal reward system, and that in the aggregate promotes the effective functioning of the organization" (Organ, 1988: 4; see also Bolino & Turnley, 2003; Smith et al., 1983). Empirical studies in this field of study hold that employees displaying organizational citizenship behavior have a disposition to "subordinate their individual interests for the good of the organization, and to take a genuine interest in its activities and overall mission" (Bolino & Turnley, 2003: 61). Furthermore, the "good of the organization" may not be narrowly defined as profit or shareholder value maximization, but may rather be identified with broader social welfare goals. For instance, managers may play a leading role in driving their firms' corporate social responsibility efforts (Swanson, 2008). Closer to our argument, the multiple bottom lines of SOEs and their hybrid transnational nature may confer upon top management teams the equivalent of the "public service ethos" found in civil service organizations (Horton, 2006; Van der Wal et al., 2008), which – in turn – may lead to organizational citizenship behavior (see Rayner et al., 2012). Indeed, several studies have shown a significant association between organizational citizenship behavior and a public service ethos in the public sector in general (de Geus et al., 2020; Ingrams, 2020) and in state-owned companies in particular (Ibrahim & Aslinda, 2013).

In addition, SOE managers' goals may be determined by what we could call "class interests." A "class-wide rationality" of corporate and state elites may result from the common social origins and educational backgrounds of business elites and top state bureaucrats in countries like France (more generally, see Useem, 1982). Similarly, SOE top management teams may be part of sociopolitical networks that include state bureaucrats (McDermott, 2004). Such networks may induce top managers to behave in a way that conforms to those networks' collective interests or norms, regardless of the managers' managerial interests (Windolf, 2002). Membership in such networks may also have framing effects, that is, it might help managers to frame their interests in a way that is consistent with their expectations of what other network members see as valuable (for the interaction between framing and network structures, see

D'Andreta et al., 2016).[10] More generally, as Scott put it, "the social construction of actors ... defines what they see as their interests" (Scott, 1995: 43).

These different goals may overlap and combine in various ways. For instance, a particular "welfare goal" consisting in sustaining employment in one specific region might be, at the same time, a "political goal" of local or state politicians who have some degree of control over the SOE's strategy. Also, SOE top management teams' goals are not static, but may change over time. Florio and colleagues (2018) find that "modern" state capitalism has shifted toward placing higher importance on economic goals over welfare or political goals, which dominated earlier forms of state-dominated economies. Indeed, their empirical study shows that a large majority (60 percent) of mergers and acquisitions by SOEs are motivated by economic goals that are related to shareholder value maximization (Florio et al., 2018). Strategic motivations – such as the development of strategic sectors – and welfare goals are secondary motivations in many cases (Florio et al., 2018: 144).

To sum up, a key contention we make in this Element is that SOE top management teams' goals and the goals pursued by state actors are not necessarily aligned. Moreover, given the multiplicity of goals that both state actors and SOE top management teams may pursue, a great variety of types and degrees of "goal misalignment" is possible, leading to a similar variety in the motivations that SOE top management teams have for seeking autonomy from state actors.

1.5 Determinants of Top Management Teams' Strategic Institutional Work: Resources, Motivation, and Scope

We posit that for an SOE to become active and try to impact its institutional environment (what organization scholars would call "performing institutional work"), three elements are necessary, each one of which is in turn shaped by institutional determinants at the three different levels of the SOE's institutional environment described earlier. The three elements are (1) the existence and the nature of the *resources* at the disposal of the SOE's top management team, which may be mobilized to pursue institutional work;[11] (2) the SOE top

---

[10] The role of frames and cognitive templates is well-known in management and organizations (Cornelissen & Werner, 2014), where they contribute, *inter alia*, to managerial sensemaking (Hahn et al., 2014). Moreover, institutional work is often seen through cognitive frames (see Bertz et al., 2024).

[11] The academic literature in management studies generally distinguishes – although not always consistently – "resources" from "capabilities," with the latter referring to the firm's routines and skills that allow it to effectively use, leverage, or mobilize resources (compare with Schnyder and Sallai, 2020). Some authors explicitly talk about "institutional capabilities" to designate organization-level routines that allow firms to mobilize resources in order to adapt to new environments (Carney et al., 2016). Here, we use the term "resources" to refer to tangible and intangible and often less firm-specific

management team's *motivation* to engage in institutional work, which relates to the congruence – or lack thereof – between the SOE top management team's goals and the institutional framework; and (3) the *scope* for the SOE's institutional work resulting from constraints imposed by the specific state–SOE governance system in which the SOE is embedded. We now discuss each of these factors before identifying their main determinants and formulating propositions.

1.5.1 Resources

The ability of SOE top management teams to engage in institutional work is determined by the type and the quantity of resources they have at their disposal (Battilana et al., 2009). The extant literature has identified various types of resources SOEs draw on when carrying out institutional work. These include financial resources, organizational resources that allow them to influence political choices (e.g. through public relations expertise), and political resources including ties with policymakers at various levels (regulatory agencies, lawmaking bodies, state shareholding managing bodies) (Boddewyn, 1994; Bonardi, 2011; Schnyder & Sallai, 2020).[12]

The availability of these resources depends, first, on firm-level characteristics – specifically, firm size and strategic value. The size of an SOE matters because larger firms can muster more financial resources and therefore display a higher capacity to perform costly political activities such as lobbying and campaign financing.[13] Furthermore, larger SOEs have greater *political clout* because their operations affect a larger number of people and, therefore, politicians' constituents (see Salamon & Siegfried, 1977). Political clout, in turn, provides SOEs with more political resources such as direct access to high-ranking public officials.

An SOE's *strategic value*, on the other hand, reflects the importance the state attributes to that company due – for instance – to the sector or industry it is active in. This importance can result from reasons related to national security, to regime survival, to economic development/wealth generation, or to broader social priorities (Hsueh, 2016). At a minimum, states tend to view defense and energy sectors as sensitive for national security and/or regime survival and

---

assets than the inherently firm-specific, non-tangible notion of "capabilities." We do consider, however, that our arguments may apply to capabilities too.

[12] Bonardi (2011) mentions other types of political resources beyond political ties based on economic assets, such as the ability of firms to threaten lay-offs. However, in the context of our framework, such broadly defined political resources might fall under the "size" or "strategic value" category.

[13] A sizeable literature exists that investigates the role of firm-level variables, especially size, in determining the extent of lobbying activities. There seems to be empirical support positively linking size to lobbying capacity. See Drope and Hansen (2006) for a review and study of the US case and Alonso and Andrews (2022) for the British case.

therefore as having strategic value. To some extent, strategic value and size can be substitutes: SOEs active in strategic sectors like defense, energy, or telecommunications will have more political clout independently of size compared to SOEs in less-sensitive sectors. This reasoning applies, for instance, to so-called national champions (Thun, 2004).

1.5.2 Scope

The second element in our framework that determines SOE institutional work is *scope*, which is defined as an SOE's ability and leeway to engage in institutional work. Scope, in turn, is determined by the SOE's resources and the specific state–SOE governance system in place that determines the relationships between the SOE and the state. Here, we define the state–SOE governance system as the system of rules, regulations, and institutions that governs the relationships between the state as owner and the SOEs in any given country. Scope comprises not only the existence in any given SOE governance system of channels SOEs can use to influence their institutional environment but also the nature of these channels. Motivation and resources are firm-level features. Scope – while partly determined by SOE resources – on the other hand also reflects the higher level of the state–SOE governance system more broadly. Indeed, regardless of the nature and amount of resources available to an SOE, its scope to perform institutional work may still be constrained or enlarged by the nature and the extent of actions at its disposal due to the nature of the state–SOE governance system.

We consider that scope partially determines an SOE's capacity to engage in actions influencing its institutional environment. Yet, scope may also influence an SOE's top management team's motivation to undertake institutional work in the first place. Thus, larger scope means more perceived opportunities for meaningful action, which in turn may motivate agents to act on their goals.

1.5.3 Motivation and Goals

The last factor in our framework that explains the likelihood of SOEs becoming active and seeking to shape their institutional environment is SOE top management teams' motivation to perform institutional work. Motivation may derive from perceived opportunities for effective institutional work and/or from the anticipated impact of (desired or envisioned) institutional change on SOE top management teams' potential goals. We already discussed the latter in Section 1.4, where we showed that the opposition or divergence of managerial interests between SOE top management teams and state actors is just one special case among a series of possible configurations of goal alignment or misalignment.

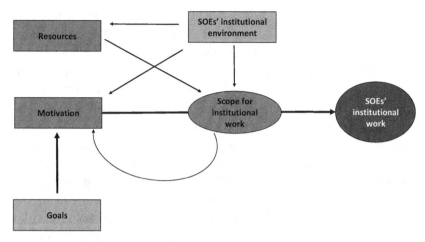

Figure 1 Determinants of SOEs' institutional work.

Within this context, our categorization of SOE top management teams' goals suggests that SOE top management teams' motivation to engage in institutional work depends on how they assess the likelihood of being able to further their goals by promoting or opposing institutional change or maintenance. Institutional change is key because SOE top management teams may consider that they can increase their ability to achieve their goals either by changing the rules of the game or by maintaining the current ones in place. Therefore, SOE top management teams' motivation to pursue institutional work depends on the goal configuration at hand and on the way in which top management teams assess the congruence of their goals with the existing institutional framework or with the proposed changes to it. Again, as hinted earlier, motivation for institutional work results from the interaction of goals and institutions at various levels. Figure 1 summarizes our model to explain the possibility that any given SOE can become active in trying to shape its institutional environment, that is, can perform institutional work.

A good illustration of the way in which scope, resources, and motivations interact to generate institutional work by an SOE is provided by Eskom, South Africa's state-owned energy utility.

1.6 An Illustration: The Eskom Case – Law, Regulation, and the Push-Back Against Renewables

In the context of the 2011 Conference of the Parties (COP17) in Durban, the South African government decided to diversify the country's electricity mix. Among other things, this change in policy meant that independent renewable power producers (IPPs) could enter the market, previously monopolized by the state provider Eskom whose energy generation capacity very largely relied on coal-fired power plants. The government introduced the Renewable Energy Independent Power Producer Procurement Programme (REIPPPP), which allows IPPs to participate in regular bid windows to become suppliers of renewable energy. Eskom operates as a monopsonist on which IPPs have to rely entirely to sell their electricity into the grid. Without access to the Eskom grid, renewable energy projects will not receive investment.

In July 2016, Eskom refused to conclude new power purchasing agreements (PPAs) with IPPs that had won preferred bidder status during the previous REIPPPP bid window (Hanto et al., 2022; Tsanova, 2017), directly and openly challenging governmental policy. Eskom's then CEO Brian Molefe refused to support the REIPPP beyond the 2018 Bid Window 4 and the programme was suspended from 2015 until 2019 as a result (Evans & Ngcuka, 2023). Molefe argued that renewable energy was making electricity more expensive and that it had "disappointed" due to immature, unreliable technology (Ngcuka, 2022).

Eskom's refusal led the South African Wind Energy Association (SAWEA) to lodge a formal complaint with the National Energy Regulator of South Africa (NERSA) in October 2016. The complaint stated that "Eskom's stance is incompatible with government policy, the law of the land, and its own licence conditions" (Yaneva, 2016: n.p.). Indeed, the minister of energy is solely responsible for decisions about new power capacity and official policy goals are to stimulate competition, diversify the energy mix, and reduce the country's carbon emissions. Eskom's refusal to sign new agreements directly challenged these goals.

Following SAWEA's complaint, in May 2017 the NERSA launched an investigation into Eskom's refusal (Tsanova, 2017). It took until April 2018 for Eskom to concede to Energy Minister Jeff Radebe's request for the SOE to sign the twenty-seven PPAs with wind and solar projects it had refused to sign since 2015 (Heap, 2018).

In its attempt to halt the energy transition and maintain its monopoly, Eskom mobilized various resources including public statements against renewables, its influence over the official regulatory process – notably through the negotiation of the multiyear price determination (MYPD) application – and informal influence over politicians. Thus, Eskom publicly blames IPPs for its financial vows and for problems with electricity supply, when in fact the MYPD allowed the SOE to negotiate energy tariffs that mean that renewable energy purchased from IPPs significantly enhances Eskom's liquidity position. Indeed, successive forward-looking MYPDs have overestimated the cost of renewable energy – which has fallen sharply in recent years – thus leading Eskom to recoup more than the actual cost from consumers (Bischof-Niemz, 2019) – also because the mechanism aimed at equilibrating over- or under-recouping of MYPD-based tariffs was suspended for several years due to political reasons.

While Eskom had to give in to Energy Minister Radebe's request, in 2019 the latter was replaced by Gwede Mantashe as minister of mineral resources and energy with an enlarged portfolio. Mantashe is more favorable to the interests of the coal industry, including Eskom – earning him the nickname Old King Coal (Davie, 2019) – and openly embraces the label "coal fundamentalist" (Evans, 2022).

Having a "coal fundamentalist" as energy minister has enabled Eskom to increase its clout and thus its resources and scope for institutional work to continue opposing competition from renewables. It has once again moved closer to a situation that South Africans refer to as "state capture" (Borath et al., 2017). Interestingly, also in 2019, the renewable sector came under pressure through suggestions by Public Enterprises Minister Pravin Gordhan that the price of renewable energy in twenty-year PPAs concluded during Bid Windows 1 and 2 in 2011 and 2012 should be renegotiated, threatening the survival of the solar industry (Bellini, 2019).

In 2019, Eskom's CEO Molefe – later arrested on corruption charges – was replaced by André De Gruyter, who resumed the RIEPPP. Tensions between the state and Eskom flared up again due to South Africa's prolonged energy crisis marked by rolling blackouts ("load shedding"). De Gruyter's tenure ended in 2022 when Mantashe accused Eskom of attempting a coup with its continuing load shedding (Gottschalk, 2023). Mantashe is quoted as saying that "[a]ny other government can be overthrown for this level of load shedding. Eskom, by not attending to load shedding, is agitating for the overthrow of the state" (Ngcuka, 2022: n.p.). This illustrates how the severe tensions between Eskom and its owner, the South African state, depend on the relationship between the Eskom CEO and the energy minister.

In short, throughout the post-2011 energy transition period, Eskom has sought to maintain the institutional environment that favored the state-owned monopolist pursuing various political and regulatory strategies to carry out its institutional work. Mike Levington of the South African Photovoltaic Industry Association (SAPVIA) hinted at a dual role of Eskom as a commercial company "that has to maintain its viability as a going concern" and as an "implementer of [the] government's energy policy" (Creamer, 2017, n.p.). Clearly, for most of the past decade Eskom has refused to play the latter role and instead used its resources to actively undermine the government's policy goals. The motivation to do so stemmed from the existential threat that the new government policy posited. Its resources to successfully oppose those policies derived from its control of the key asset – the energy grid. Its scope to perform institutional work in order to oppose changes to the institutional environment ebbed and flowed with political changes, but remained considerable due to its close ties with the state even when the political juncture was less favorable. Taken together, the Eskom case illustrates how motivation, resources, and scope are important factors determining SOEs' ability to favor or oppose institutional change. Sections 2–4 identify the key factors that determine the motivation, resources, and scope of institutional work by SOEs.

2 The Macro Environment

We consider two features of the macro-institutional environment of SOEs that potentially affect wide swathes of every economy – and are particularly liable to influence SOEs' institutional work. One is the financial system. In this section, we look at one specific configuration of modern financial systems, namely financial repression, and how the existence and operation of financial repression in various economies affects SOE top management teams' institutional work. Then, we turn to examine how industrial policy, broadly defined, affects SOE top management teams' institutional work.

2.1 Financial Repression

Financial repression can be helpfully defined as "keep[ing] nominal interest rates lower than would otherwise prevail" (Reinhart, 2012).[14] To be more exact, financial repression includes interest rate controls on both bank loans and deposits with spreads sufficiently large to maintain bank viability and below-market interest rates (Park & Patrick, 2013; Pettis, 2013).[15] Importantly, this chapter makes no normative critique or defense of financial repression, unlike critics (Hoffmann, 2019; McKinnon, 1973[16]) and proponents of such policies (Chari & Henry, 2004; Reinhart, 2012). We simply follow past scholarship in observing that governments have often leveraged financial repression to steer capital into priority sectors. Developing and industrializing economies thus have employed financial repression to try to spur economic development and industrialization throughout the twentieth century, including, at its most extreme, Nazi Germany (Tooze, 2006), but also Japan, South Korea, and Taiwan in the latter half of the twentieth century (Patrick

---

[14] This section defines financial repression according to its classic formulations (McKinnon, 1973; Shaw, 1973). This definition is narrower and thereby more exact than the broader one used by some scholars, who include various kinds of state regulation and state interference in the definition of financial intermediation (Roubini & Sala-i-Martin, 1995).

[15] Financial repression can also include "high, lowly compensated reserve requirements" for banks (Claeys et al., 2010).

[16] Note that in later life McKinnon expressed a much more positive opinion of financial repression in the case of China; this is based on discussions one of the authors had with him in 2006.

& Park, 1994), contemporary China (Park & Patrick, 2013; Pettis, 2013), and several European countries such as France, Italy, and Spain (Loriaux et al., 1997).

Where financial repression is an important feature of the macro-institutional landscape, it can shape both motivation for SOEs' institutional work and the types and quantities of resources available to SOEs to engage in institutional work. Of course, the impact of financial repression on SOE top management teams is contingent upon how much the actors pursuing financial repression (typically governments) prioritize state ownership as the vehicle for their financial repression-fueled investment push. While South Korea and Japan leveraged financial repression for industrial investment in their developmental heydays, neither country focused investment on nonfinancial SOEs. Singapore has had financial repression and many SOEs (called government-linked corporations), but the focus of its industrial strategy was on multinationals, not local firms (Yeung, 2016). Thus, financial repression in these countries did not have much impact on institutional work by SOE top management teams, as private (foreign, in Singapore's case) conglomerates rather than SOEs were the main beneficiaries of financial repression.

In contrast, China has had even stronger financial repression (measured in terms of the transfer of wealth from household savers to industrial investors as a percentage of gross domestic product) than South Korea or Japan (Pettis, 2013), and has targeted SOEs as one of the main vehicles for industrial investment. China's SOE-oriented financial repression has had several important effects on SOE top management teams.[17] Financial repression has given the requisite resources for China's SOE top managers to pursue strategic empire-building. The goal is to grow to too-big-to-fail size in the eyes of the state leadership and financial repression provides the cheap credit to do just that (Fuller, 2016; Huang, 2003, 2008; McMahon, 2018; Pettis, 2013). Moreover, funneling financial repression through state-owned banks whose mandate is to privilege SOEs in lending, such as the absence of a requirement for collaterals for SOEs (O'Connor, 2000), presents SOEs with a powerful lever over government through the threat of non-performing loans. Thus, in China and Vietnam, with their similar systems of SOE-centric financial repression, SOEs borrow large sums, creating systemic importance for themselves that locks the government into a mutual-hostage situation with the SOEs. Governments can't reform the financial repression system and thus financially discipline the SOEs without creating financial turmoil. This systemic importance secures for large SOEs a privileged position in the financial system.

---

[17] In addition to top management teams enriching themselves via the riches financial repression steered their way (Huang 2003).

Within such a pro-SOE financial repression system, Chinese SOEs strategically maneuver to enlarge their mutual dependence with the state. Chinese SOEs have pursued institutional work in the form of trying to push institutional maintenance, namely, the maintenance of the system of SOE-oriented financial repression. Since the announcement of major reforms to end the system of financial repression and the concomitant lending bias toward SOEs at the Third Plenum of the 18th Communist Party of China (CPC) Central Committee in November 2013, top leaders such as former Premier Li Keqiang alluded to SOEs blocking reforms (Fuller, 2016; McMahon, 2018; Minzner, 2018). Even one of the major optimists who earlier heralded the rise of China's private economy in place of the SOEs, Nicholas Lardy (2014), now admits that the financial system continues to be heavily biased toward supporting SOEs (Lardy, 2019). The state has still not allowed the deposit rates to move freely and continues to keep them artificially low (Zhang, 2022).

Taiwan also had an SOE-centric economy featuring financial repression in the 1950s and 1960s. However, Taiwan's financial repression was lighter (less credit shifted from households to firms and at less generous interest rates) than what occurred in Korea, Japan, and China (Park & Patrick, 2013; Pettis, 2013) and less biased toward SOEs and away from supporting other firms than China (Fields, 1995; Patrick & Park, 1994). The Taiwanese more minimalist case of financial repression allows us to understand under what conditions financial repression increases resources and motivations for SOEs to engage in institutional work. Taiwan pursued financial repression from the 1950s into the 1980s (Patrick & Park, 1994).

State-owned firms comprised almost half (49 percent) of Taiwan's manufacturing value-added in 1951. Private industry began to blossom in the 1960s and the state share of manufacturing value-added was below 20 percent by 1976. Nevertheless, the state in the 1970s still invested in large SOEs in shipbuilding, steel, petrochemicals, and autos (Chu, 2017; Hsueh et al., 2001). Despite the SOEs' former economic and policy dominance, private firms rather than SOEs played the lead role in most of these sectors by the end of the 1980s. Even China Steel, arguably the most successful of the big SOEs to emerge from Taiwan's 1970s industrial policies, could not stop the trade liberalization in steel; nor did it succeed in acquiring Taiwan's private "minimills." Instead, China Steel faced new private competitors (Noble, 1998). Similarly, in the mid-1980s, private mid-stream petrochemical producers managed to get permission to invest in their own upstream, naphtha cracker plant in competition with state monopoly producer China Petroleum Corporation (Hsueh et al., 2001).

The nature of financial repression in Taiwan explains why SOEs there were not able to engage in institutional work to block privatization despite their efforts to do just that (Hsueh et al., 2001; Noble, 1998). With less generous credit and less pro-SOE bias in lending, Taiwanese SOEs could not acquire the resources to become systematically important to the economy and thus the government. Taiwan's financial system never offered such low interest rates, so Taiwan's SOEs were less tied to financial repression, had fewer resources, and were more market-facing than Chinese SOEs. Under these conditions, their incentives to engage in institutional work to maintain the financial repression were much weaker.

Based on these observations of SOEs in economies featuring financial repression, our argument can be summed up with the following lesson:

> *Lesson #1: The more SOE-oriented the financial repression is, the more such financial repression enhances the motivation and ability of SOE top management teams to pursue institutional work.*

2.2 Industrial Policy

Following Warwick (2013: 16), we define industrial policy as "any type of intervention or government policy that attempts to improve the business environment or to alter the structure of economic activity toward sectors, technologies, or tasks that are expected to offer better prospects for economic growth or societal welfare than would occur in the absence of such intervention." Historically, state ownership has played a large role in industrial policy. In the immediate post–World War II period, state ownership, in conjunction with economic planning, was a key industrial policy strategy in advanced economies (Nude, 2010). Starting in the 1970s and 1980s, the role of SOEs diminished (Toninelli & Toninelli, 2000). While many juxtaposed regulatory states and industrial policy pursuing states, others recognized that regulatory states still had industrial policies (Thatcher, 2014; Vogel, 1996). In the case of SOEs, partial privatization and sale of shares in SOEs in advanced economies enabled SOEs to internationalize, expand into new markets, and establish alliances with private firms (Thatcher, 2014).

Industrial policy, to the extent that it utilizes SOEs as the targeted firms, enhances the resource endowments and the motivation for institutional work. In post-apartheid South Africa, for instance, state-owned electricity utility Eskom escaped the privatization of other SOEs because of the importance of its infrastructure to achieving the industry policy goals of the new ANC government – that is, universal electrification of the country and modernization of the electricity networks (Ballim, 2023). More recently, Datang Telecommunications in China took advantage of SOE-centric policies in the telecommunications and semiconductor industries to accumulate resources and motivation for institutional work.

Embracing the state's 3G TD-SCDMA (time division – synchronous code division multiple access) technology strategy allowed Datang to survive in a period when its market share had fallen precipitously low. These SOE-friendly industrial policies also incentivized Datang to push for further industrial policies. The firm then used these resources to play an active role in investing in the semiconductor industry and concomitantly to push the state to create even more ambitious, SOE-friendly industrial policies (Fuller, 2016).

Another interesting case of industrial policy enhancing SOEs' role and thereby increasing SOEs' resources for institutional work is Taiwan. While the country had turned away from emphasizing SOEs by the 1980s, the Taiwanese state was forced to create new SOEs for its emerging semiconductor industry when private capital proved very reluctant to commit more than paltry amounts to this new high-priority – if high-risk – sector. The primary SOE vehicle for this sector was TSMC, which was founded in 1987. From the beginning, the state was a reluctant investor with state bureaucrats as concerned about avoiding blame for a potentially expensive failure as they were with fostering this new sector. Thus, the original plan was for a minority state share and a foreign partner. In the end, the government provided the majority of the funding and Philips was the foreign partner with 27 percent ownership. The plan was always to lower the state's ownership exposure to this firm even as the state prioritized Taiwan's development of a semiconductor industry (Fuller, 2007). From the beginning, the government gave Morris Chang, the founder of TSMC, great managerial leeway even if the state also imposed much penny-pinching in the initial funding. Over time, the state share of TSMC fell as planned and came into line with the reality of private management of the firm. At the same time, Taiwan continued to prioritize the semiconductor sector because it became spectacularly successful thanks to TSMC, by far the largest Taiwanese semiconductor firm. For its part, TSMC used the state policies to grow in size and, starting in the mid-1990s, began to throw its weight around. It blocked attempts by the state to pursue new technology transfer initiatives in the industry by refusing to join them. Without TSMC signing on, it was hard for the state to justify the expense of such initiatives and TSMC was not interested because it now had the financial wherewithal to pursue research independently. Additionally, TSMC successfully campaigned against a state-organized bailout of the memory chip industry; TSMC saw that bailout as throwing good money after bad – money that TSMC thought could be better used supporting TSMC (Fuller, 2018). The problem the state faced was that TSMC, through success and continued state support, had become both the symbol of state industrial policy success and so large and important for Taiwan's economy that the government could not afford for TSMC to go into decline. By the second decade of the 2000s, the tide had decisively turned in the behemoth TSMC's favor. When the state was slow to disburse subsidies, TSMC threatened to move its newest factories abroad. The state then immediately complied. When TSMC did not like some minor comment from the minister of science and technology, he was immediately fired (Fuller 2018, 2021). Through the state's semiconductor-prioritizing industrial policy, TSMC was able to maneuver itself into being *the* indispensable company for Taiwan's economy. Its institutional work has admittedly not been broad – it cares only to make sure that the business environment and substantial government support go its way – but it has been effective and even decisive. As one state bureaucrat told one of this Element's authors, the lesson learned for state bureaucrats is to never talk about TSMC in public.

But industrial policy is not necessarily "friendly" to SOEs. In the case of "hostile" industrial policy, however, SOEs might even draw stronger motivation to undertake institutional work. This can be illustrated by the complex relationship between French state-owned utility EDF and its state shareholder. A 2010 law forced EDF, which holds a monopoly over nuclear-powered electricity generation, to sell part (25 percent) of that electricity each year to (private and state-owned) competitors at a price well below the retail market rate – those competitors then sold EDF-generated electricity directly to consumers, at market prices.[18] In January 2022 the French government, which held, by then, an 84 percent stake in the utility, decided to amend the 2010 arrangement to force EDF to sell a greater chunk of its electricity to competitors – a decision that had an immediate impact on the utility's financial position and on the share price (Le Monde with AFP, 2022). This "hostile" decision, motivated both by the government's desire to cut retail electricity prices ahead of important national elections and by the deepening of an industrial policy mostly predicated on opening up electricity markets to competitors, was not easily accepted by EDF or EDF's non-state stakeholders. For instance, unions immediately reacted to the January 2022 decision by organizing protests. More interestingly, a year and a half later (in the summer of 2023), while EDF had been fully nationalized, EDF was seen lobbying European law-makers to weigh in on tense negotiations surrounding the future European regulations of "clean" energy, at cross-purposes with the French state (Malingre, 2023).

---

[18] The arrangement, called ARENH (*accès régulé à l'électricité nucléaire historique*), was put in place by Law n.2010–1488, and was due to last fifteen years. It was motivated by the European-wide efforts to liberalize energy markets.

These few examples illustrate the strong links tying SOEs' potential agency to industrial policy, which we can sum up in the following lesson:

Lesson #2: The more active an industrial policy incorporating SOEs is, the greater the motivations and the scope for SOE top management teams' institutional work are.

3 The State–SOE Governance System

Beyond the macro-level determinants of SOE institutional work discussed in Section 2, a second important set of determinants, which we call the *state–SOE governance system*, is situated at the meso level. Our aim here is to unbundle this system and show how it may relate to the likelihood of SOE top management teams undertaking strategically important institutional work.

In the literature on state capitalism, state control over SOEs broadly corresponds to what some authors call "effective ownership," which is defined as the "amalgam of both the level of ownership as well as the means to exercise control over the entity" (Cuervo-Cazurra et al., 2014: 924). In line with this view, we identify the institutional underpinnings of state control with the state–SOE governance system, which encompasses state ownership patterns, the governance of state shareholdings, and the non-ownership links tying SOE top management teams to the state apparatus. In our framework, the state–SOE governance system affects all three determinants of SOEs' institutional work: resources, scope, and motivations.

3.1 Patterns of State Ownership

We know from the existing literature on state capitalism and the available data that there is significant variation in the *degree* of state ownership across countries and among SOEs in individual countries. This acknowledgment has led Musacchio and Lazzarini, in a series of works, to contrast "Leviathan as a minority investor" with "Leviathan as a majority investor" (Inoué et al., 2013; Lazzarini & Musacchio, 2018; Lazzarini et al., 2021; Musacchio & Lazzarini, 2014; Musacchio et al., 2015). This insight constitutes an important nuance to the "traditional" view of SOEs as non-corporate parts of the state bureaucracy or firms whose capital is entirely owned by the state. In addition, Musacchio and Lazzarini broaden the scope of state capitalism, which they define as "widespread influence of the government in the economy, either by owning majority or minority equity positions in companies or by providing subsidized credit and/ or other privileges to private companies" (Musacchio & Lazzarini, 2014: 2). This view is shared by the World Bank, which proposes to expand the notion of state ownership beyond the "conventional" notion of state ownership as majority control of the state to include firms with minority, indirect, and subnational equity ownership by the state – a larger set of firms the World Bank labels "businesses of the state" (Dall'Olio et al., 2022; World Bank, 2023). Of course, this has implications for measurement of state ownership[19] and recognition of its actual significance. In the 91 countries covered by the World Bank's Global Database of Businesses of the State, World Bank economists found 76,000 enterprises with state equity shares of 10 percent or more (World Bank, 2023).[20]

Beyond measurement issues, however, this broader conceptualization of state ownership has two significant implications for our understanding of its political and economic consequences – and, more narrowly for our purpose here, its impact on SOE agency: first, the degrees of state ownership should be viewed on a continuum even as, for empirical reasons, researchers may be driven to turn this continuum into a series of discrete classes (for instance 10 percent to 49.99 percent equity shares, 50 percent to 99.9 percent, 100 percent); second, it is not only the degree of state ownership that varies but the directness of ownership links, too, that is, whether state ownership is direct or indirect, exerted through other state-owned firms or their subsidiaries.[21] Together, the degree of state ownership and the directness of the ownership links form what we call *patterns of state ownership*.

However, variations in patterns of state ownership and the effects such patterns have on the likelihood of SOE institutional work interact with two additional important characteristics of state ownership. First, state ownership embodies a multiplicity of strategic goals, which have a crucial bearing on potential misalignments of goals between (broadly defined) state actors, on the one hand, and SOE top management teams, on the other (see also Coutant et al., 2021; Estrin & Gregorič, 2022).

This multiplicity of goals interacts with the heterogeneity of industries or sectors where SOEs operate. Minority equity shares may have very different meanings across sectors. In the defense and aeronautic industry, for instance, often deemed strategic by the state shareholder, minority equity shares may

---

[19] As the World Bank rightly notes, previously widely used definitions of SOEs, such as the OECD's ("any corporate entity recognised by national law as an enterprise, and in which the state exercises ownership" – OECD, 2015), which appear to cast a wide net, were actually quite narrow when applied to select data and cases (World Bank, 2023; see also, more broadly, Dall'Olio et al., 2022, for a methodological discussion).

[20] In line with the broader view of state ownership adopted by the World Bank, from the point of view of data collection and analysis, an entity is considered an SOE if, inter alia, it is "controlled by government units or by other public corporations, proxied by a level of direct or indirect (*i.e.* subsidiaries) participation of above 10%" (Dall'Olio et al., 2022: 6).

[21] Not to be confused with the direct or indirect *governance* structure of state shareholdings, which we will turn to next.

correspond with high degrees of state control and monitoring, embodied by the state shareholder's willingness to actively use its minority share to influence the firm's strategies. More generally, golden shares have historically been a popular tool by which the state shareholder attempts to retain control over partially privatized firms (Grundmann & Möslein, 2004; see also Bałtowski & Kozarzewski, 2016, for the Polish case). In other cases, however, minority ownership may indicate the state attributing less strategic importance to that sector (compare with Hsueh, 2016).

Second, patterns of state ownership have a history. Therefore, it might be more accurate to speak of trajectories of state ownership rather than levels. Such trajectories may stay hidden under the surface of even very extensive cross-sectional, cross-country studies, such as the one performed by the World Bank with the Global Database on Businesses of the State, which is available for one data point only, namely, 2019. Again, minority equity shares might reflect a new investment (in broad terms) of the state into a private company and a new sector, as, for instance, most of the cases analyzed by Musacchio and Lazzarini under the "Leviathan as minority shareholder" label (Musacchio & Lazzarini, 2014); or they may result from partial privatization processes revealing the gradual withdrawal of the state from established public firms and/or sectors (such as in the European rail industry: see Lethbridge, 2020). Minority state ownership may hence be the result of two opposing trends or dynamics.

This variation in the patterns of state ownership matters. As empirical evidence increasingly shows, different degrees of state ownership may generate effects on SOEs' strategic behavior (Musacchio et al., 2015). Arreola and Bandeira-de-Mello (2018) and Kalasin and colleagues (2020) show how different degrees of state ownership affect SOEs' internationalization. According to Inoué and colleagues (2013), varying degrees of state ownership translate into different degrees of firm-level performance. Furthermore, as demonstrated by Cui and Jiang (2012), different degrees of state ownership are also associated with varied degrees and types of institutional pressure experienced by SOEs. It is thus reasonable to expect that the degree of state ownership is likely to affect SOE top management teams' willingness and capacity to perform institutional work.

However, for several reasons the relationship between state ownership and SOE behavior and/or performance can be expected to be nonlinear. Firstly, degrees of state ownership are not necessarily correlated with the extent of state control in a linear fashion. The relationship between the two is, ultimately, a matter of empirical assessment on a case-by-case basis. For instance, as the Organisation for Economic Co-operation and Development (OECD) judiciously points out, "whether a 'golden share' amounts to control depends on the extent of the powers it confers on the state" (OECD, 2015: 14). As argued earlier in this section, degrees of state ownership interact, firstly, with various ownership-related characteristics and, secondly, with governance structures (see further below).

Second, state control generates contradictory effects. On the one hand, one may follow Musacchio and Lazzarini (2014), for whom the causal relationship between state ownership and SOE performance runs like this: varying degrees of state ownership determine degrees of state control, which affect the ability of SOE managers to pursue objectives of their own, assumed to be economic in nature, and to diverge from the state actors' non-economic interests. In this view, lower degrees of ownership (and therefore control, in Musacchio and Lazzarini's view [Lazzarini & Musacchio, 2018; Musacchio & Lazzarini, 2012, 2014]) are associated with better performance, because lower control enables SOE top management teams to evade political interference. Thus, *decreasing* state ownership will favor SOEs' strategic autonomy, to the benefit of firm performance.

On the other hand, state ownership also generates resources – in particular, access to non-equity funding by the state or by other SOEs. These resources might be viewed through a (normatively) negative lens. Thus, according to Inoué and colleagues, state ownership facilitates capital expenditure in SOEs exposed to funding constraints – for instance because of a defective institutional environment (Inoué et al., 2013). Even low degrees of state ownership carry non-equity advantages: as Musacchio and Lazzarini point out – like majority state control – minority state shareholdings "may actually benefit politically connected capitalists rather than [non-state-owned] financially constrained firms" (Musacchio & Lazzarini, 2014: 5), which may not be economically efficient as finance is allocated based on political connections, not economic opportunity to invest. A case in point is the vast financial support provided by governments to SOEs during the COVID-19 crisis in 2020.[22] The French finance minister, for instance, declared early on that the French state was willing to support state-owned Airbus through a broad range of mechanisms, including greater access to export finance but also labor subsidies to prevent massive layoffs (*"chômage partiel"*) and "helping airline companies to renew their fleets."[23] Conversely, if state ownership comes with access to financial and nonfinancial resources, in some cases – where state-owned firms have profitable

---

[22] There is no evidence yet that such support was disproportionately in favor of SOEs as against privately owned enterprises. However, a recent study on Britain found a strong positive relationship between firms' political connections and the likelihood of receiving state support during the COVID-19 pandemic (Wood et al., 2023).

[23] See the Reuters article at https://investir.lesechos.fr/actu-des-valeurs/la-vie-des-actions/la-france-prete-a-aider-totalement-et-massivement-airbus-le-maire-1836321 (accessed 2 November 2024). Of course, the airline company that the French minister was thinking of was another SOE, Air France.

investment opportunities – *increasing* state ownership may be associated with increasing firm-level performance.

Similarly, Kalasin and colleagues (2020) find an "S-shaped" relationship between state ownership and internationalization of SOEs: low degrees of state ownership are associated with low internationalization; as state ownership increases, internationalization increases, until it decreases again with high degrees of state ownership. According to Kalasin and colleagues (2020), this S-shaped relationship is due to two opposite effects of state ownership: a "hindering hand" effect, whereby increasing state ownership compounds multilevel agency problems and thus prevents internationalization strategies; and a "helping hand" effect, whereby increasing state ownership provides SOEs with increasing resources. This argument is very much in line with the agency framework proposed by Musacchio, Lazzarini, and colleagues (Inoué et al., 2013; Lazzarini & Musacchio, 2018). Overall, then, the net effect of state ownership is theoretically indeterminate and can only be assessed empirically (Lazzarini & Musacchio, 2018).

In our context of SOEs' strategies to influence their institutional environment, we also expect that varying degrees of state ownership will lead to different likelihoods of SOEs performing institutional work. However, our explanations differ from those offered by Lazzarini and Musacchio (2018; Musacchio & Lazzarini, 2012, 2014) and by Kalasin and colleagues (2020) in two respects.

Firstly, as argued already in this section, how the degree of state ownership translates into *state control* depends on a combination of factors: the directness of the state ownership (i.e., whether ownership is direct or indirect through intermediary owners); the historical trajectories of the state ownership; the multiple goals of the state ownership; and the interactions among all three elements. In other words, it is not the same, from the point of view of state control/SOE autonomy, to have an SOE with a minority share as a result of partial privatization with a goal to raise money for the state, and a different firm with the same degree of ownership as a result of partial bailout or nationalization for strategic reasons.

Secondly, SOEs' strategies to influence their institutional environment are not exclusively driven by attempts to challenge the government's goals or to change the institutions in a way that better fits an SOE top management team's goals or interests. In reality, SOEs may equally well use institutional work to maintain the existing institutional framework, that is, by performing institutional work that strengthens the government's policy goals (see Micelotta & Washington, 2013). This is even more the case if, as we argued in Section 1, the goals driving SOE top management teams are more multifaceted than is assumed by the agency view, which posits that agents (the SOE top management teams) will tend to pursue different interests (and certainly not political ones) from the principals (the state). In contrast, we do not assume an a priori divergence or alignment of interests between state bureaucrats and SOE top management teams but see it as an empirical question.

Consequently, an increased degree of state ownership does not necessarily reduce managers' scope to further their own interests and therefore create the motivation to seek institutional change. Rather, we argue that increasing state ownership does not necessarily act as a deterrent preventing SOE top management teams' (institutional) action, as held by Cui and Jiang (2012), but may generate increasing political *resources* that will enable SOEs' institutional strategies. For example, in the case of SMIC (Semiconductor Manufacturing International Corporation), China's largest integrated circuit manufacturer, the central government and the Shanghai government held only minority stakes. As a consequence, despite SMIC's large size, it was not prioritized by either the central government or the Shanghai government and therefore had little influence over China's integrated circuit industry policies (Fuller, 2016). Only after the state effectively took over SMIC's board did the state place SMIC front and center in its semiconductor industrial policies, but at the same time being front and center of the state's industrial policy encouraged autonomous empire-building in the form of acquisitions by SMIC's top management team (Fuller, 2019). Here, higher levels of local and/or central government ownership may have enhanced – not reduced – the scope for the SOE top management team's institutional work.

In sum, we argue that greater state ownership, other things being equal, provides SOE top management teams with greater scope for institutional work due to there being greater political resources via two mechanisms: Increasing the degrees of state ownership increases the formal and informal interactions between SOE top management teams and the state and thus enhances top management teams' political resources by expanding informal and formal ties to other state elites. Simultaneously, increasing state ownership also increases SOEs' economic and strategic value in the eyes of the state. Thus, SOE top management teams can wield this enhanced valuation as a political resource.

Conversely, scope decreases with the degree of state control, which also increases with state ownership. A good illustration of this is France's Engie, which is partially owned by the French state (with a 24 percent equity stake) and which is much more proactive with respect to regulatory reform than was GDF (Gaz de France), its fully state-owned predecessor, which may have had more political resources but was also more closely state-controlled, reducing its scope for successful institutional work, a fact illustrated by the recent turnover at the helm of the company.[24] The ambiguous role played by the French state – as the dominant minority shareholder of Engie – is an additional illustration of the contradictory effects of minority state ownership on resources and scope (Marin, 2020).

The degree of state ownership affects not only the SOE top management team's scope for institutional work but also its *motivation* to undertake it. The motivation of SOE top management teams to influence their institutional environment is affected by degrees of state ownership through its relationship with scope. The larger the scope for institutional work, the greater the perceived opportunities for successful institutional work (Battilana et al., 2009; Dorado, 2005) and hence the motivation to become active. Therefore, like scope, the motivation of SOE top management teams to perform institutional work will rise with increasing degrees of state ownership, until the high degree of state ownership starts reducing scope and, consequently, disincentivizes SOE top management teams from seeking to act in order to change or maintain their institutional framework. This corresponds with Boies' (1989) argument about large (private) American firms' political activities, whereby a firm's interest in engaging in corporate political activity is compounded by the extent and depth of that firm's relationship with the state apparatus (Boies, 1989).

The relationship between state ownership and SOE institutional work may be altered by the presence of shareholders other than states co-owning SOEs (Musacchio et al., 2015). The presence of non-state institutional investors, for instance, may provide SOE top management teams with both scope and motivation (or pressures) to diverge from state goals (see Grosman et al., 2024).

The implication of the discussion in this section about the degree of state ownership is that the commonplace view that higher levels of state ownership mean less SOE autonomy and hence less SOE strategic action needs to be revised. Instead, we point out that higher levels of state ownership also mean higher levels of political resources and heightened strategic value. This may be counterbalanced, however, by the enhanced state control over SOEs that comes with larger ownership stakes. Increasing state ownership (from a relatively low level) will also increase SOE top management teams' motivation to undertake institutional work – as opportunities and resources are initially greater – but very high levels of state ownership may see their motivation decline again. In

---

[24] Here the logic of our argument is not fundamentally dissimilar from the one put forward by Lazzarini and Musacchio (2018) whereby the good performance of SOEs across the world (across their panel) may be attributed to the extra resources provided by state ownership. In Lazzarini and Musacchio's framework, these resources (which they call "protection" and "rents" rather than political resources) mitigate the misalignment of state and SOE goals, and thus attenuate the negative impact of state ownership on SOE performance. Our framework, on the other hand, does not conceive of top management teams' goals as a priori misaligned with state bureaucrats' goals.

practice, this implies that the most active SOEs in terms of shaping their institutional environments can be expected to be those that have a moderate level of state ownership, which maximizes SOE top management teams' resources and motivation to become active.

3.2 Governance of State Shareholdings

Beyond degrees and patterns of ownership, state–SOE relations are governed through specific governance structures that determine the lines of command and authority. Indeed, the academic literature has shown that the actual impact of ownership is predicated upon the actual forms of governance of state shareholdings (Estrin & Gregorič, 2022), which we turn to in this section.

Corporate governance structures can be defined as systems of rules that allocate rights and responsibilities to various stakeholders and participants in the firm (Aguilera & Jackson, 2003). In the case of SOEs, a key component of the governance system is the *lines of authority* they establish with different state actors. Lines of authority are distinct from ownership ties; SOEs are embedded in structures of control and supervision that may or may not be underpinned by ownership ties. Thus, central banks or ministries of finance can have oversight rights over SOEs regardless of whether or not they have an ownership stake in those SOEs.

Like ownership patterns, there is great variation in these structures, which may be more or less centralized within the state apparatus and more or less fragmented across state agencies (OECD, 2020, 2021; World Bank, 2014). These structural components of the state–SOE governance system determine what we label the "structural" autonomy of SOEs vis-à-vis state actors and agencies.

International financial institutions usually classify SOE governance structures into a limited number of types (OECD, 2020; World Bank, 2014). In particular, the OECD considers five types of governance structure: a centralized model, a coordinating agency model, a dual ownership model, a "twin track" model, and a decentralized ownership model (OECD, 2020). In the traditionally widespread centralized model,[25] all state shareholdings are managed by a single entity, which can be a ministry (traditionally the ministry of finance, like in Colombia and South Korea) or a body that is autonomous from the government – such as the French Government Shareholding Agency (*Agence des Participations de l'État,* or APE)[26] or Chile's *Sistema de Empresas Publicas* (Public Enterprise System).

---

[25] According to the OECD (2020), the centralized model ("with or without exceptions") prevails in almost half of the thirty-two countries surveyed in its study, which includes most advanced economies (with the exception of Australia, Canada, Spain, and the United States) and a small group of middle-income economies (without China or India, for instance).

[26] In the French case, two other state-owned or public entities, beyond APE, play a key role in managing state shareholdings, especially in the financial industry (*Caisse des Dépôts et*

In the twin track model, there are two main shareholding management entities, each with its portfolio of individual SOEs. This model is distinct from the dual ownership model, where two ministries ("or high-level public institutions" – OECD, 2020: 11) jointly exercise their ownership rights over SOEs – usually with the ministry of finance exercising some overarching oversight over financial performance, like in Brazil or the Czech Republic.

In the coordinating agency model – also called the "advisory" model by the World Bank (2014) – state shareholdings are dispersed across several decision units or ministries, but one central coordinating agency plays an advisory role on technical and operational issues and may take on a monitoring role as well. This is the case, for instance, with United Kingdom Government Investments (UKGI).

Finally, in the decentralized model – the second-most-widespread type of state shareholdings governance structure, according to the OECD – various "line ministries" directly control and manage their ownership rights over their own portfolio of SOEs. This is the governance structure prevalent in Argentina and Japan, for instance.

Recent reform guidelines published by the OECD and the World Bank have encouraged a move away from the decentralized model toward the fully centralized one, with the coordinating agency model constituting an acceptable second-best solution (OECD, 2015). For our purpose, the key difference between these models or types of governance is whether the designated state unit or units govern the SOE through indirect financial means or through direct intervention into the management of the SOE. The international organizations' preference for the centralized model stems from the belief that such a structure will isolate SOEs from undue direct political interference from politicians, making SOEs more focused on financial goals and thus more efficient. Indeed, it is expected that such "agencification" – whereby ownership and control over SOEs are transferred from bureaus within the state bureaucracy to autonomous agencies – will lead to stronger incentives for SOE top management teams to pursue and deliver on economic goals (Vining et al., 2015).

The indirect, financial model of governance has two contradictory effects on the likelihood of SOEs adopting strategies geared toward influencing their institutional environments: This structure implies a heightened financial and commercial accountability toward the asset managing entity. Thus, SOEs will be pushed to more narrowly focus on economic and financial goals. At the same time, asset management entities have more limited mandates and goals than

---

Consignations and BPI France), bringing it closer to a twin track or, rather, "triplet track" structure.

ministries and fewer resources at their disposal. From the SOE perspective, replacing ties to active management entities with ties to asset management entities therefore implies a decrease in the resources that SOEs can draw on to perform institutional work. According to our model, this will negatively affect SOEs' scope to perform institutional work.

However, the indirect, financial governance structure also means that SOEs are politically more autonomous from the state as it becomes harder for politicians to control SOEs directly (World Bank, 2014: 79). Indeed, "agencification" has been shown to lead to increased managerial discretion toward the state (Vining et al., 2015). We would therefore expect that SOEs embedded in a governance structure that isolates them from direct state control will have more scope to pursue institutional work, especially when their goals diverge from the government's goals.

At the same time, a shift from decentralized government control to direct agency control may in many cases entail a decrease in the multiplicity of government principals (see, however, the Paraguayan case mentioned a little later). Since the existence of multiple principals is associated in the literature with greater SOE autonomy (see Musacchio & Pineda Ayerbe, 2018), the later shift should decrease SOE top management teams' scope for institutional strategies. Overall, however, we expect the effect of isolation of SOEs from direct state control to be stronger than the effect of a potential reduction in the number of principals, because the type of principal an agencificated system relies on can be expected to reduce SOE scope less than other types of principal.

In France, for instance, all state shareholdings are managed by a specialized entity, the *Agence des Participations de l'État* (APE, cited above), created in 2004, which is autonomous from the Treasury. Of course, although an autonomous entity, APE has very close ties to the Treasury, in terms both of its governance and of its staffing: The *Cour des Comptes* – France's supreme public accounting body – found in a 2017 report that the four most senior positions at APE were held by members of the Treasury. Yet, the objectives of APE are very different from the very traditional hierarchical relationships characterizing the Treasury–SOE relationships in the postwar era. APE's official mission is to use equity ties to sustain "national champions" or companies representing the "national interest" – that is, per APE's official mission statement to "embody the shareholder State" by investing into companies "deemed, strategic by the state," "to stabilize their equity or accompany them in their development or transformation."[27] For French SOEs, this 2004 change

---

[27] Source: APE mission statement, as spelled out on the agency's official website: www.economie.gouv.fr/agence-participations-etat/notre-mission-statement (accessed 19 December 2023).

in governance meant greater insulation from the more political goals of the Treasury, thus increasing their structural autonomy.

Emerging and developing economies, too, have been reforming their SOE governance structures in recent years, along the lines suggested by international financial institutions, with potential implications for SOE scope for institutional work. Thus, Paraguay implemented a reform in 2008 – under the maverick president Fernando Lugo – that centralized control over SOE and removed control from ministries to transfer it to an inter-ministerial SOE Council supported by an SOE Monitoring Unit (World Bank, 2014: 268–269). While political influence in this system is still potentially strong, because ministries remain represented on the Council, SOEs are more insulated from political interference by individual ministries and may benefit from more political leeway due to the multiplication of potentially divergent political interests represented on the SOE Council.

In short, beyond the international financial institutions' focus on efficiency and performance, our analysis suggests that changes to SOE–state governance structures have important implications for SOE top management teams' ability to influence their institutional environment and thus play a quasi-political role. Those SOEs that are governed by a centralized state agency through indirect, financial mechanisms rather than by a state agency with direct managerial control will at the same time have more structural autonomy and therefore more scope to pursue institutional work, even while they have fewer resources to do so. Which effect will dominate (reduced resources or increased political autonomy) is contingent on other factors, including the political integration of SOE elites with other state elites and the "nomenklatura" system in each polity (see Section 3.3).

3.3 Other Non-ownership Ties

State–SOE relations do not start and end with ownership ties, mediated by governance structures. Other, non-equity relationships tie SOEs to the state apparatus, and also affect the scope of SOEs' ability to influence their institutional environment. The multiplicity and the heterogenous nature of ties binding SOEs to state agencies and bureaucrats have been attracting increasing attention from scholars (see Cuervo-Cazurra et al., 2014; Musacchio & Lazzarini, 2014), who focus on debt (subsidized credit), board seats, regulation, and other, softer forms of control such as staffing and contracts. Here, we distinguish between two broad kinds of non-ownership state–SOE ties: non-equity financial ties between SOEs and state agencies and the social-political ties linking SOE top management teams to state agents.

3.3.1 Non-equity Financial Ties

Regarding the former, increasing attention has been paid to non-equity funding to SOEs. Musacchio and Lazzarini (2014), among others, consider non-equity financing by the state (through subsidized loans in particular) to be a defining characteristic of the "Leviathan as minority investor" model (see also Cull & Xu, 2003). However, non-funding ties to the state matter as well. We call these institutional ties to distinguish them from the social and personal ties that SOE top management teams have with state agents. These ties are additional to equity ownership and encompass auditing and monitoring (not always exercised by the state shareholder) as well as contractual ties with the state administration.

In France, for instance, the steering and supervisory roles of APE as shareholder are compounded by the financial and economic controlling function exerted by yet another autonomous body, the *Contrôle Général économique et financier* (CGefi), whose mission is to audit public organizations – including firms with the state as an equity shareholder.

Considering contractual ties, one may cite the five-year contract (called *Contrat de Régulation Economique*) signed by ADP (Aéroports de Paris, where the French state is a majority shareholder, with 50.63 percent of equity), which operates the three largest airports of the Paris region (Paris-Charles de Gaulle, Paris-Orly, Paris-Le Bourget), with the French state (i.e., the ministry in charge of civil aviation). Such contracts, regulated by civil transportation laws, set up certain "regulated activities" where agreed pricing and rates of return can be applied.

3.3.2 Social-Political Ties

Social-political ties[28] have been historically significant in the trajectories of state capitalism. For instance, according to Schneider (1992), personal networks played a key role in determining the political strategies of business in South America during the twentieth century. These ties were especially significant in the case of Mexico, Chile, and Colombia, where business associations formed the locus of tight, informal ties between businesses and politicians, enhancing the collective action of businesses with regard to government policy and regulation. More recent evidence in various countries shows the persistence of strong political ties between elected state officials and SOE top managers, which produces significant effects on the professional careers of SOE managers.

---

[28] We use this term, rather than the narrower "political ties" focus of the literature, to indicate the broader range of relationships between SOE top management teams and state actors, including common educational backgrounds and common social origins.

Betz and Pond (2023), for instance, show that politically connected individuals are more likely to manage state-owned firms. For China, Leutert and Vortherms (2021) have shown how integration into a political patronage network increases SOE managers' chance of staying in office. In Poland, Szarzec and colleagues (2022) found a much higher turnover of board positions at SOE firms than in private firms – a finding illustrated by the fate of the CEO of PKN Orlen, a Polish state-owned oil refinery giant, whose ascent to the helm of the utility was widely seen as the direct outcome of his political closeness to the previous president, and who was ousted a few weeks after a new political majority took office (Reuters, 2024). Therefore, as Okhmatovskiy argues, our understanding of both the mechanisms of state control and the scope for SOE managers' agency would gain from a shift of focus "from the mere fact of state ownership to the politically motivated intervention in firms' corporate governance" (Okhmatovskiy, 2010: 1021).

There is, however, an ongoing debate as to the impact that such social-political ties have on SOEs' strategy and performance. On the one hand, the economic literature – particularly agency theory – has often treated social-political ties as constraints negatively affecting SOEs' operations and bottom lines. In this perspective, state control carries with it political goals that are alien to the business objectives of the firm, thereby hampering these objectives and damaging the firm's performance (Shirley & Walsh, 2000; Shleifer & Vishny, 1998).

However, research in management has significantly qualified this picture, underscoring the benefits that companies can draw from ties with the state. Indeed, such ties can increase performance by permitting access to resources, information, and preferential treatment (Johnson & Mitton, 2003; Lester et al., 2008; Xin & Pearce, 1996). In a study of Russian banks, Okhmatovskiy (2010) argues that social-political ties create opportunities and constraints; in particular, ties with the government may be important for firms to influence policies, although they may not help in accessing resources. Thus, the effects of social-political ties on firm performance will be based on the balance of the costs and benefits of those ties. Sun and colleagues (2010) add that the value of social-political ties can change dramatically as a country's institutional system moves toward a more market-based system. A recent study of Indonesia shows contradictory findings: social-political ties may both increase SOE top management teams' compliance with the private demands of their government-linked principals *and* be leveraged to resist such compliance (Aprilyianti et al., 2023). In a meta-analysis of literature on state ownership, political connections, and SOEs' financial performance, Tihanyi and colleagues find no strong relationship between state ownership and performance and no relationship at all between political connection and financial performance (Tihanyi et al., 2019).

However, the same study shows that both state ownership and political connections have strongly significant effects on strategies. In short, political embeddedness does have important, if complex, implications for firms.

There is also a great variation in the legal status and degree of state embeddedness of SOE staff: from SOEs employees as civil servants to a complete separation between the careers of state employees and those of SOE employees (see, e.g., Grindle, 2010; Liang et al., 2015). This variation is reflected in the diverse appointment paths experienced by SOE top management teams (see earlier in this section). In addition, social-political ties can take several forms, from interchangeable career paths (revolving doors) to common educational backgrounds. Various studies have pointed to the links between political and managerial careers as a key component of state capitalism in China (see, in particular, Boisot & Child, 1988; Fan et al., 2007; Groves et al., 1995; Lin et al., 2013). In France, a high proportion of senior staff and top managers at the largest French firms have historically been trained in the prestigious "Grandes écoles" system that works as a training center for future civil servants. According to one study, in 2010 41 percent of top managers in French SOEs still belonged to the "*grands corps,*" (Dudouet & Joly, 2010) – a form of elite networks of public servants institutionalized within the French administration. This peculiar form of socialization ensures common views and informal communication channels between state authorities and SOEs.

In a number of state-planned and formerly state-planned economies, the state often attempts to exert strict control over SOEs' top management teams via bureaucratic procedures concerning personnel or "nomenklatura," which derives from the Russian term for the list of important posts in government and industry to be filled by Communist Party members in the Soviet Union.

For example, in China nomenklatura refers to lists of positions directly appointed by the CPC's Central Organization Department (Leutert, 2018). When this nomenklatura system functions in terms of its Leninist intent, the party-state exerts strong control over the appointment and monitoring of the top management teams in SOEs. In such situations, one would expect the SOE top management teams to have little space in which to pursue institutional strategies. However, if the nomenklatura system is fractured or the SOEs can somehow buck the control of the nomenklatura system through playing the party-state organ in charge of nomenklatura against other party-state organizations in control of SOEs, the SOEs can create space to pursue institutional strategies. For example, among China's central government SOEs, some are formally under the control of SASAC (the State-owned Assets Supervision and Administration Commission [of the State Council]), but the Organization Department and the SOE top managers' own accumulated rank and power can be used to thwart control by SASAC or any other authority (McGregor, 2012; Walter & Howie, 2011).

It is important to draw a clear distinction between the functioning of the nomenklatura system and the level of integration of SOE management into the wider political elite. A functioning nomenklatura system means that the party-state maintains effective control over the SOE management it appoints. However, integration of the SOE managers into the political elite has often led to the breakdown of nomenklatura control either as SOE managers outrank their nominal supervisory agencies or as their connections to top leaders thwart such control.

Therefore, there is an indeterminate relationship between the political embeddedness of the top management team and motivation for undertaking institutional work. On the one hand, the more embedded an SOE top management team is in the political system, the more it has the political resources and enhanced scope for institutional work. Enhanced scope feeds into enhanced motivation. On the other hand, the greater the political embeddedness of the top management team, the less likely it is that the top management team will be motivated to engage in institutional work because the top management team will be more likely to embrace whatever beliefs about institutional creation, maintenance, or disruption the ruling political elite has. When in ideological agreement with the political leadership, SOE top management teams will be passive followers rather than active champions of institutional work.

Overall, the discussion in this section suggests that the embeddedness of SOE managers in state structures via formal (e.g. appointment) and informal (social-political ties) is key to understanding whether and how SOE top management teams may seek to be and be successful at shaping or reshaping their institutional environment. Again, the relationship between the two is complex and ultimately probably an empirical question, but our study provides insights into which factors will shape SOE institutional strategy.

> *Lesson #3: The integration of SOEs into the state–SOE governance system has ambiguous (indeterminate) effects on SOEs' likelihood to do institutional work. On the one hand, the greater the integration into the state apparatus, the greater the resources that SOEs can draw on for institutional work. On the other hand, greater state–SOE integration can also generate more control, which may simultaneously decrease the scope and increase the motivation for institutional work.*

4 Industry Characteristics

Drawing on the industrial organization-inspired works of the classic external approach to strategy in management studies (compare with Porter, 2008), we now turn to sector-level factors that influence SOEs' ability to shape their institutional environment. Vertically integrated firms can reduce competition in their industry (i.e., increase their market power) by threatening suppliers and even buyers with backward or forward integration. This threat is more credible when a firm is already quite vertically integrated. As a parallel to this firm-level strategy view, firms have greater clout in their respective economy the more market power they exercise. This clout is, in turn, enhanced in vertically integrated industries because the firms tend to be bigger in such industries and firm size increases clout. Industrial policy interacts with this tendency for vertical integration in that, under conditions conducive to vertical integration, the state will favor a select few national champions in sectors that favor vertical integration (Gerschenkron, 1962; Nolan, 2001) and thus provide the targets of such industrial policies with even more resources. The resources that SOEs seek for institutional strategies are shaped by the characteristics of their industries. In temporal periods and sectors where vertical integration has competitive advantage, SOEs would seek to add resources to build greater scale economies and make their very size and scale of strategic value to the government.

In contrast, the global value chain (GVC) literature emphasizes that forces for segmentation/de-verticalization/disaggregation of the value chain often exist in specific industries (Arndt & Kierzkowski, 2001; Berger, 2005; Fuller et al., 2003; Gereffi et al., 2005; Langlois, 2003; Thun, 2007). In disaggregated value chains, firms, often relatively small-scale ones, interact with many other firms along the value chain and specialize in narrow segments or functions along that chain (Fuller, 2013; Thun, 2007). Vertically disintegrated value chains generally favor such vertically specialized firms. Vertically specialized firms do not typically have the large scale and strategic weight of vertically integrated behemoths, so, to the extent that SOEs are competitive in these sectors, they will also have to be relatively small vertical specialists. Such small, vertical specialists lack the heft of abundant resources and strategic value to do institutional work effectively.

The GVC and industry studies scholarship tends to assume that the relative advantage of vertical specialization varies by sector or subsector (Berger, 2005; Fuller et al., 2003; Gereffi et al., 2005; Thun, 2007). However, it is plausible to argue that different periods of time favor either vertical integration or vertical specialization. Thus, the emphasis on industrial policy-cum-planning favored in the early post–World War II decades may have been a rational reaction to the advantages of Fordism at that time before such advantages dissipated in the 1970s (Piore & Sabel, 1984). Scholars of industrial change (Gereffi et al., 2005) posit that a trifecta of high complexity of information, transaction costs, and asset specificity will encourage vertical integration. Functioning in a tipping point fashion, the combination of these factors could push industries from de-verticalization to vertical integration or vice versa. Note that Lesson #4, which follows, does not incorporate the three factors outlined here because the assumption is that there is some tipping point at which vertical integration/specialization becomes the dominant competitive mode of organization.

Scholars have noted that certain time periods favor vertical integration or greater vertical specialization (Langlois, 2003), although some debate how strong these cross-sectoral forces for vertical integration/specialization are (compare with Newman & Zysman, 2006). During periods of vertical integration dominance, SOEs should possess relatively stronger capabilities for institutional work. Historically, the dominance of vertical integration and industrial concentration coincided with the strategic value and logic of using SOEs to pursue industrial development. Plausibly, this conjunction came about because governments in these periods of highly concentrated industrial capacity felt it politically safer to have these large companies directly under government control (Amatori, 1997; Hsueh et al., 2001). When vertical specialization becomes more competitive, these state-owned industrial behemoths look outmoded, expensive, and pointless. Consequently, SOEs lose strategic value and suffer from scale diseconomies. For example, French, Italian, and Taiwanese models of vertical integration predicated in large part on SOEs in the 1950s and 1960s began to face pressures during the 1970s (Hsueh et al., 2001; Piore & Sabel, 1984; Zysman, 1977).

This argument can be summarized with the following lesson:

Lesson #4: Periods and sectors favoring vertical integration lead to larger and more strategically valuable SOEs, which in turn gives SOE top management teams greater ability to pursue institutional work.

The faster the pace of technical change (incorporating both fast product life cycles and fast clockspeeds[29]) in an industry, the more likely it is that disruptive innovation undermining incumbents' advantages will occur (Christensen 1997; Fine 1998, 2000; Utterback & Suarez 1993). Therefore, incumbent SOEs in such industries will be in greater danger of having their strategic value diminish in the eyes of state bureaucrats or politicians and/or find themselves with fewer

---

[29] The industrial clockspeed is the pace of technical change controlling for product complexity (Fine, 1998, 2000). It is important to note that clockspeed is *not* a measure of the technological intensity of the industry, as some industries with slow clockspeeds, such as the commercial aircraft industry with its product technology generations of ten to twenty years, are technologically intensive (Fine, 1998).

resources. The SOEs in such fast-paced industries will consequently face greater resource constraints for institutional work.

There are confounding factors. Fast clockspeeds also have influence via mechanisms featured in other propositions. Fast clockspeeds can boost vertical specialization (Fine, 1998; Steil et al., 2002). However, vertical specialization critically depends on standardization with digital interfaces to lower the transaction costs between firms across a vertically specialized value chain (Christensen, 1997). State industrial policy is also likely to be less effective in fast-paced sectors as state policy may lag badly behind changing industry demands (Schmitz, 2007). Therefore, industrial policy in fast-paced sectors should prove less amenable to the kind of resource accumulation that enables SOEs to pursue institutional work. Conversely, institutional feedback mechanisms from trends favoring vertical integration could affect industrial policy incorporating SOEs.

We therefore formulate the following lesson:

> *Lesson #5: The faster the pace of technical change in a given industry is, the lower the ability for SOE top management teams to pursue institutional work is.*

The case of Brazilian SOE Embraer illustrates the relevance of political drivers for our propositions on industry characteristics. While the industry trends were not necessarily trending toward complete vertical integration, especially for a firm in the developing world that needed critical parts and partners from countries with advanced aerospace industries, the Brazilian state in the form of the military in 1969 created and then heavily promoted Embraer during the military dictatorship (1964–1985) for national security reasons. Consequently, the state emphasized that Embraer should be as vertically integrated as possible. This rigid focus on national security somewhat limited Embraer's ability to seek out commercial partners and opportunities abroad (Maculan, 2013). However, when the Brazilian economy began to falter in the late 1980s, government financial backing for Embraer also began to falter. The threat of bankruptcy led to Embraer's privatization in 1994 where the state retained only golden shares to prevent foreign firms from buying it out.

Ultimately, changing politics allowed a move away from state fixation on the merits of vertical integration and consequently liberated Embraer to pursue a somewhat more vertically specialized approach drawing upon the expertise of advanced partners abroad. From 1994 to 2000, Embraer embraced foreign partners and market opportunities to develop the regional jet-powered aircraft ERJ1354/145 that propelled the firm into becoming the third largest regional jet manufacturer in the world (Maculan, 2013).

Additionally, SOEs may use their scope for institutional work to counter governments' efforts to de-emphasize existing technologies and sectors and the SOEs associated with them. Thus, the case of Eskom in South Africa illustrates that SOE top management teams can use institutional work to obstruct the development of new technologies so as to maintain their monopoly over old ones. In this case, for years, Eskom successfully blocked renewable energy producers from selling electricity into the grid in order to protect its coal-based electricity plants.

5 Combining Determinants: An Overall Framework to Account for SOEs' Institutional Work

5.1 The Overall Framework

Our approach underscores the importance of simultaneously assessing factors at all three levels of institutional determinants to truly understand each case of institutional work by individual SOEs. This is in line with configurational academic approaches to institutions, which see them as bundles rather than scalar variables as more mainstream economic approaches suggest (Jackson & Deeg, 2008). Given the multiplicity of factors affecting the likelihood of SOE top management teams engaging in institutional work, we expect significant variation both across and within countries. In Section 5.2 we illustrate this diversity by drawing on the example of a country not normally associated with state ownership, namely, the USA.

5.2 An Illustration: Institutional Work by Powerful SOEs in North America – Fannie Mae and Freddie Mac

These days when people think of SOEs they often think about post-socialist economies and state capitalist ones. However, even the bastion of liberal capitalism, the United States, continues to have powerful SOEs – principally housing mortgage giants Federal National Mortgage Association (Fannie Mae)[30] and Federal Home Loan Mortgage Corporation (Freddie Mac). How did the top management teams of these two SOEs manage to navigate the decades of "neoliberalism" from Reagan to Trump to grow and even prosper (from the narrow point of view of the corporate insiders)?

At the time of their bailout to the tune of US$191.5 billion during the global financial crisis, Fannie Mae and Freddie Mac were government-sponsored enterprises (GSEs) with hybrid structures, being both listed, for-profit

---

[30] By the 1980s, Fannie Mae was already the third largest American corporation in terms of assets (Moss et al., 2009).

companies and federally chartered (Wiggins et al., 2021). Despite the common trajectories of these two SOEs recently, their origins are different. The federal government established Fannie Mae in 1938 during the New Deal to rescue the housing market and increase home ownership during the Great Depression. Freddie Mac was established in 1970 at the tail-end of the New Deal political era when even Republicans such as Nixon were in favor of social spending, even if only for reasons of political expediency.

The federal government created Fannie Mae in 1938 in order to ensure enough of a secondary market for Federal Housing Administration (FHA)–backed mortgages with Fannie Mae's money coming directly from the Treasury (Moss et al., 2009). Even though Fannie Mae was not authorized to intervene in the primary market (i.e., issue mortgages), it in effect did engage in mission creep by intervening in the primary market by issuing pre-commitments to buy mortgages (Moss et al., 2009). The problem from the point of view of Treasury budgetary considerations was that mortgage issuers were very eager to get Fannie Mae pre-commitments as they could charge processing fees, while the risk went almost entirely to the FHA and Fannie Mae. Thus, mortgage issuers tried to get as many Fannie Mae pre-commitments as they could handle, driving up costs for the Treasury. The Treasury and financial organizations involved in the secondary market wanted to privatize Fannie Mae, but others feared that breaking Fannie Mae's government backing would badly impact the housing market. Thus, in 1954, the government split the difference. Fannie Mae was reorganized as a hybrid entity owned by the Treasury Department and the many home-loan entities with which Fannie Mae did business.

In 1968 under President Johnson, the government exited its ownership from Fannie Mae as technical budgetary issues pushed privatization,[31] but it retained important control rights and other links. The US government retained the right to appoint five of Fannie Mae's fifteen board members and the American president could remove any of the board members, including the ten voted on by common stock shareholders. The Department of Housing and Urban Development became the main government regulator of Fannie Mae as it had the right to approve any securities issue and any above-limit[32] mortgage purchases by Fannie Mae.

---

[31] President Johnson's budgetary commission recommended that Fannie Mae's secondary market actions be counted in the federal budget, but this accounting change would have increased official federal spending by 1.5 percent so Johnson viewed privatization of this "new" federal spending as politically expedient (Moss et al., 2009).

[32] The limit was fifteen times Fannie Mae's capital and surplus as of legislation in 1966. Prior to this, the limit was ten times (Moss et al., 2009).

In 1970, the federal government created Federal Home Loan Mortgage Corporation (Freddie Mac) because savings and loans associations lobbied the government to have a secondary market purchaser of mortgages they issued as Fannie Mae mainly did this for banks (Carr & Anacker, 2014). Some viewed Freddie Mac as adding competition in a market where Fannie Mae was dominant.

Within four years of Fannie Mae's quasi-privatization (privatization of ownership if not control) in 1968, Fannie Mae had turned from a purchaser of FHA and Veterans Administration (VA)–backed mortgages to purchasing mainly conventional mortgages. In the 1970s, Fannie Mae ran into trouble with its post-quasi-privatization method of fundraising – selling non-mortgage-backed debt securities – since it bought fixed-term mortgages but interest rates on its shorter-term debt fluctuated. Thus, Fannie Mae in the early 1980s turned to selling pass-throughs where mortgage payments went directly to buyers of these mortgage-backed securities. The chairman of Fannie Mae, David Maxwell, led this charge and the change to buying new adjustable-rate mortgages, both of which brought Fannie Mae's costs down and forced the lifespan and the yield of assets and liabilities into greater sync. The main constraint on Fannie Mae's entrepreneurship was the federal government preventing Fannie Mae from buying jumbo mortgages with large unpaid principals (Moss et al., 2009).

It was generally assumed by investors that Fannie Mae and Freddie Mac had implicit federal government guarantees backing them. The Reagan administration in fact targeted this assumed implicit government guarantee as the reason to fully privatize Fannie Mae and Freddie Mac. However, ultimately no progress was made on this issue during the Reagan administration.

Inspired by the Reagan administration's attempt to privatize, a renewed push was made in 1992 to better regulate these two SOEs[33] and thus restrain the financial risk they exposed the government to, but Fannie Mae and Freddie Mac lobbied successfully to water down the Federal Housing Enterprises Financial Safety and Soundness Act and its newly created regulator, the Office of Federal Housing Enterprise Oversight (OFHEO), which was under the Department of Housing and Urban Development (HUD) (Lincoln, 2013). This lobbying marks the beginning of extensive institutional work activity by both Fannie Mae and Freddie Mac. Both firms began to expend significant resources to try to keep federal regulations on these housing SOEs very loose. As Thompson (2009) documented, Fannie Mae and Freddie Mac pursued a four-pronged political campaign to keep regulation on them very light. First, they gave direct

---

[33] More specifically, Fannie Mae and Freddie Mac are considered, in US law, as GSEs. Such enterprises are created by US Congress; while not necessarily state-owned, their federal charters are widely viewed as being very similar to state equity ownership ties in other contexts.

contributions to members of Congress amounting to US$19.3 million from 1990 to 2008. Second, they pursued lobbying of Congress to the tune of US$170 million from 1998 to 2008. Third, they manipulated the justifications for social housing and housing needs of minorities to rally support for light regulation from Democrats in Congress. For example, the Fannie Mae Foundation was a big backer of the Congressional Black Caucus (CBC) and in return CBC members were prominent defenders of Fannie Mae against attempts to impose stricter regulations. Finally, these SOEs repeatedly challenged their regulator, the OFHEO, often with the help of Congressional allies.

These attempts at institutional work in terms of maintaining the light regulatory framework of the SOEs were generally successful until the global financial crisis, despite setbacks for certain institutional work activities. The Federal Election Commission (FEC) in 2006 gave Freddie Mac the largest fine the FEC had ever imposed due to Freddie Mac's illegal campaign contributions. Fannie Mae executives were also caught by the OFHEO increasing their bonuses and compensation between 1998 and 2004 through accounting irregularities. Given the OFHEO's reputation for light touch regulation that led to this accounting mess, various members of Congress, mainly Republicans, tried to pass bills to bring these SOEs under tighter Treasury-led regulation. Fannie Mae and Freddie Mac spent considerable resources to successfully fight these measures in Congress (Thompson, 2009).

The inability to regulate these SOEs while they were using implicit government guarantees in mortgage markets led the two firms to accumulate $5.3 trillion in mortgages and guarantees and $1.7 trillion in debt once the real estate markets collapsed in 2008 (Wiggins et al., 2021). The government took over the firms with just under 80 percent ownership and created a new regulator under the Treasury with robust powers, the Federal Housing Finance Agency (FHFA), to replace the toothless OFHEO. The FHFA has kept the two firms in conservatorship since 2008, where the FHFA has completely controlled the firms in place of boards and with any dividends going to the Treasury until 2019 when the firms' bailout debts to the government had been already paid off. At the time of writing, the government still has the two firms in conservatorship and demands that each firm build a capital reserve of US$300 billion from earnings before the government will consider allowing the firms to leave conservatorship (Weinstein, 2024).

The institutional work undertaken by Fannie Mae and Freddie Mac prior to their collapse in the global financial crisis embodies several of the claims made in this Element. Fannie Mae and Freddie Mac had limited state ownership and as such more scope for institutional work. Similarly, their embedding in a state–SOE governance system based on indirect supervision – rather than direct control – by the HUD and the Treasury gave them more structural autonomy and thus wider scope for institutional work. However, in contrast to the assumption that reduced state ownership decreases the resources that SOE top management teams have available for institutional work, they were able to take advantage of changes in the financial system and federal policies to encourage off-budget social housing financing, in order to become too-big-too-fail firms. Of course, the fact that Fannie Mae and Freddie Mac were at the center of public financing for home ownership for decades was a form of political integration and conferred upon them political resources that they exploited to preserve their light regulatory environment, a form of institutional maintenance, until the global financial crisis brought them down.

Conclusion

The Impact of SOEs' Institutional Work: Institutional Maintenance, Change, and Stability

Our main intent in this Element was to present a framework capable of better explaining the institutional aspects of the "paradox of embedded agency" characterizing SOEs – that is, the fact that SOEs, albeit more deeply embedded than private firms in the web of state rules and power relations, are also motivated and able to perform autonomous strategic actions that are aimed at maintaining or altering that web – namely, SOEs' institutional environment. Understanding SOEs' institutional work seems like an increasingly important endeavor, given the so-called return of the state and hence the increasing numbers of SOEs among the world's largest companies. It provides a corrective to the view that SOEs are simply an instrument of the state and thus enhances our understanding of not just state capitalist economies but a wide range of economic systems where SOEs exist.

The production of such a framework required, in our view, four different, complementary tasks, drawing on various academic literatures. Firstly, we conceptualized SOEs' agency toward their institutional environment as "strategically important institutional work," drawing on the institutional work literature in management and organization studies. This framing acknowledges that any actor and any level of the organization may perform institutional work, and that we limit ourselves to the sort of strategically – rather than operationally – important instances that are typically the remit of top management teams. Secondly, drawing on several related social science literatures (particularly the literatures on managerial behavior and on political resources), we identified the immediate determinants of SOEs' institutional work: motivation, resources, and scope. Thirdly, we drew on comparative institutional analysis – especially as it is developed within the so-called comparative capitalisms literature, which is in turn closely associated with historical institutionalism, to identify the main *institutional* determinants of SOEs' institutional work, at the macro, meso, and sectoral levels. Fourth, and finally, we made inferences about the causal effects that such institutional determinants have on the likelihood of SOE top management teams performing institutional work to shape the institutional framework in which they are embedded.

Overall, our framework deciphers the peculiar paradox of embedded agency faced by SOEs by shedding light on the mechanisms through which various types of institutions may activate specific catalysts for SOEs to engage in institutional work. That two-way, intricate relationship is not symmetrical: some of the institutions identified as determinants of SOEs' institutional work are less likely than others to be the target of the latter: for instance, patterns of ownership, which play such an important role in determining the scope, resources, and motivation to perform institutional work, are rarely within the reach of SOEs' top management teams, in contrast to specific technical regulations or strategic industrial policy, for instance. Our core message, however, is in line with the observation made by Zietsma and Lawrence that "embedded agency is not paradoxical but simply dependent on complex institutional structures and heterogenous forms of agency" (Zietsma & Lawrence, 2010: 218).

Yet our work steers away from the kind of analysis usually associated with institutional work, in at least three respects: firstly, we choose to focus on institutional work by firm-level actors *from the point of view of the firm* (i.e., the SOE) *itself*. This reflects our assumption, spelled out in Section 1, that the actions undertaken by SOE top management teams to shape their institutional environment are taken on behalf of the firm. This contrasts with the choice of many studies in the institutional work literature that focus on groups of actors who do not necessarily act in the name of a specific class of organization. Our approach, on the other hand, ties in with a recent literature that focuses on the business enterprise – state-owned, in our case – as an actor in its own right that may be driven by internal "activists" performing institutional work. Oftentimes, such internal activists are lower-level employees in the organizational hierarchy (Girschik, 2020), but the literature has also started to focus on the role of top-level managers – including CEOs as political actors within the firm – for better or worse – turning the whole corporation into a political actor (Feix & Wernicke, 2023).

Secondly, and relatedly, we adopt what may be called a political-economy frame to analyze the catalysts leading to SOEs' institutional work. This is in contrast, again, with the sociology of practice influencing much scholarly work on institutional work (Hampel et al., 2017).

Thirdly, we focus on the whole institutional environment in which SOEs operate, including large-scale, macro institutions and meso-level factors typically overlooked by the literature on institutional work (Hampel et al., 2017). We also analyze SOEs' institutional work with respect to potential conflicts with state agents.

Ultimately, indeed, we see *state–SOE goal misalignment* as a powerful motivation for SOE top management teams to undertake purposeful action to shape their institutional environment. This action may result in gradual institutional change, where the status quo pursued by state actors goes against the goals pursued by SOE top management teams, and where the latter have both the scope and the resources for successful institutional work. Alternatively, this action may lead to institutional maintenance, when state actors pursue institutional change and SOE top management teams successfully oppose it.

Implications of SOEs' Institutional Work for the Institutional (In)stability of State Capitalism

Our framework offers no predictions of *actual* institutional change or stability. We make no claim here about the systemic effects of SOEs' institutional work on the institutions targeted by SOEs. Indeed, our analysis is focused on the determinants of individual firms' behavior; it has a clear micro focus, even as we carefully delineate the role that macro- and meso-level institutions play in determining the likelihood of such agency taking place, and as we ultimately aim to explain not any kind of agency but agency that aims to maintain or change the institutions surrounding SOEs. This focus explains why we cannot claim here to offer accounts of systemic change within national varieties of (state) capitalism.

Indeed, we embrace the historical institutional view that although institutional change is driven by purposeful actors, the actual outcomes of institutional change depend on politics and coalitions, which makes it highly contingent and hence subject to the specific historical circumstances in which it occurs (Pierson, 2004; Thelen, 2004, 2014).[34] As Thelen puts it, "institutions are the object of ongoing political contestation, and changes in the political coalitions on which institutions rest are what drive changes in the form institutions take and the functions they perform in politics and society" (Thelen, 2004: 31).

This is why our predictions concerning SOEs' behavior (see Table 2) cannot be directly connected to predicting the types of institutional change that would result from changes in the coalitional foundations of particular institutions or institutional systems, changes themselves resulting from the interaction of the

---

[34] As Peter Hall argued, collective action problems "loom large . . . in the processes of institutional change" (Hall, 2010: 204).

Table 2 SOEs' institutional work and its direction

Goal alignment	State intention	SOEs' scope for IW	SOEs' resources for IW	Likelihood of IW	Direction
State–SOE goal alignment	Stable	High	High	Low	Institutional stability
		High	Low		
		Low	High		
		Low	Low		
State–SOE goal alignment	Reform	High	High	Low	Institutional change
		High	Low		
		Low	High		
		Low	Low		
State–SOE goal misalignment	Stable	High	High	High	Institutional change
		High	Low	Moderate	Institutional change/stability
		Low	High	Low	Institutional stability
		Low	Low		
State–SOE goal misalignment	Reform	High	High	High	Institutional maintenance
		High	Low	Moderate	Institutional change/stability
		Low	High	Low	Institutional change
		Low	Low		

Note: IW = institutional work.

group of actors we focus on (SOE top management teams) with other actors within and outside their institutional environment. This does not mean that this "coalitional step" of the process of institutional change does not affect SOEs' motivation to pursue institutional change. Coalitional dynamics – which involve the characteristics of the political context, such as the strength of veto points – can directly affect the effectiveness of the institutional agency pursued by individual SOEs. However, they cannot, in our perspective, be conceived as *directly influencing* SOEs' motivation to act – unless one conceptualizes SOEs as fully rational actors able to form rational expectations about their strategic interactions with other actors in order to reach a certain result (a certain type of institutional change). The latter view is clearly incompatible with an institutionalist's account – as Mahoney and Thelen point out, "actors face information-processing limitations and certainly cannot anticipate all of the future situations in which rules written now will be implemented later" (Mahoney & Thelen, 2010: 12).

At the same time, our framework may usefully complement historical institutionalist accounts and contribute to a better understanding of institutional change within state capitalism. What is missing in the historical institutionalist framework is a nuanced incorporation of individual agents – such as business firms in general, and SOEs in particular – into the model of actor-centered institutional change. Such a model should indeed incorporate a mid-range theory of these important actors' motivations, scope, and resources to act, which our framework provides. Instead, historical institutionalist scholars focus on "change agents."[35] From the historical institutionalist perspective, what matters for institutional change is the selection process of those change agents that, once they form politically successful coalitions, will make (incremental) change happen. In other words, what the historical institutionalist framework does is formulate predictions "concerning the kinds of environments in which different agents are likely to emerge and thrive" (Mahoney & Thelen, 2010: 28).[36]

Those agents, however, are mostly "macro agents," in line with the traditional political-economy focus on interest groups: business associations, labor unions, political parties. What we argue here, by contrast, is that individual firms and important actors within them may be important vectors of institutional change as

---

[35] Mahoney and Thelen write that "change agents become the intervening step through which the character of institutional rules and political context do their causal work" (Mahoney & Thelen, 2010: 28).

[36] In Mahoney and Thelen's framework, both the characteristics of the political context and the characteristics of the particular institution shape the process of institutional change by "shap[ing] the type of dominant change agent that is likely to emerge and flourish in any specific institutional context, and the kinds of strategies this agent is likely to pursue to effect change" (Mahoney & Thelen, 2010: 15).

well. As far as state capitalism is concerned, in particular, SOEs should be reconsidered as important "change/maintenance agents" in their own right. To understand this, institutional theory in organization studies provides useful theoretical and conceptual tools. That is not to deny the importance of such firm-level actors' interactions with other actors and in the context of coalitional power plays, but it enhances the importance of their agency beyond merely being represented by higher-level collective actors.

This firm-centered view does not bring us back to the actor-centered functionalism criticized by HIs for its determinism and unrealistic rationalist assumptions.[37] Indeed, our argument that SOEs' likelihood to pursue institutional change or maintenance (through institutional work) is in large part institutionally determined immunizes us from the temptation to find rational individual foundations for institutional change.

However, we suggest that "macro" accounts of institutional change brought about by shifts in coalitional politics could incorporate more micro- and meso-level analyses of institutional work by SOEs as potential change or maintenance agents. To do that, one could build on our framework models of interaction or coalition-building among SOEs, and between SOEs and other domestic (business firms, employers' associations, trade unions, civil society organizations . . .) and international actors.

Implications of SOEs' Agency for the Outcomes of State Capitalism

In addition to our contribution to the ongoing debates in the social sciences around institutional change within contemporary capitalism, this Element aims to contribute to the comparative dynamics of state capitalism. State capitalism is a complex, multifaceted, and evolving phenomenon (Grosman et al., 2023; Musacchio et al., 2015; Wright et al., 2022).

Outside of a few early attempts to "bring the state back in" (Rueschemeyer et al., 1985), much of the management literature as well as the recent comparative capitalism literature in political economy has evolved in the context of the retreat of the state. This has left scholars ill-equipped to conceptualize the "return of the state" as an economic actor that we have witnessed in the past decades in the shadow of trends in Western countries toward privatization, liberalization, and depoliticization of the economy. As a result, attempts to account for the role of the

---

[37] Paul Pierson defines actor-centered functionalism as "the claim that a particular institution exists because it is expected to serve the interests of those who created it" (Pierson, 2004: 105). By contrast, Pierson argues, "Actors may be instrumental and farsighted but have such multiple and diverse goals that institutional functioning cannot easily be derived from the preferences of designers. Alternatively, actors may not be instrumental [and/or] farsighted" (Pierson, 2004: 108).

state in twenty-first-century capitalism have been rather caricatural, for example reducing the role of the state in state capitalism exclusively to one of ownership (Kurlantzick, 2016) or providing a conceptualization so coarse that countries as diverse as China and Norway are lumped together under one type (Situ et al., 2020).

There are many ways in which to improve on such crude understandings of the state's role in state capitalism (see, e.g., Alami & Dixon, 2020; Schnyder & Sallai, 2020). In this Element, we focused on one specific way in which our understanding of state capitalism can be refined, namely, by theorizing in a much more fine-grained way the relationship between the state and one of its most important agents for economic activity, namely, the SOE. Rather than conceiving of the capitalist state as a monolithic entity, we see it as an assemblage of agencies and actors who are tied together through a complex set of personal and impersonal, formal and informal relationships that are constantly subject to maintenance and change, involving state actors at various levels of the state bureaucracy. These relationships vary across contexts and over time. Theorizing the factors that determine these relationships allows us to provide a framework that is flexible and applicable to a wide range of empirical cases of states and of capitalism and enhances our understanding of the nature and evolution of this type of modern capitalism.

In particular, our framework offers insights into the inherent instability of state capitalism. Indeed, contrary to the perception that state capitalist systems are more stable than other types of capitalism due to the sheer dominance of the state as a coercive apparatus, change is omnipresent here, too. Importantly, we do not simply draw on the historical institutionalist argument about the pervasiveness of incremental change due to institutional adaptation and shifts in support coalitions (Thelen, 2004). Rather, one key implication of our framework is that incremental change, within state capitalism, is endogenous to state–SOE relations and constitutive of the peculiar "paradox of embedded agency" characterizing SOEs. For instance, high levels of state ownership, while apparently guaranteeing the stability of the state's control over substantial sectors of the economy, may create both a high motivation and enough resources for SOEs to seek institutional change. Paradoxically, this is how stability and the state's might could contain the seeds of change.[38] This implication of our framework chimes with earlier insights into state-dominated systems, namely, developmental states. Evans (1995) notes that the developmental state's use of (privately

---

[38] Our argument runs parallel with the more political-economy-focused thesis formulated by Nolke and colleagues, whereby, in state capitalism, disenfranchised groups will tend to demand more political participation that will "eventually clash with a 'cronyist' economic coordination mechanism" at the heart of the system (Nölke et al., 2019: 4).

owned) national champions to achieve its industrial policy goals creates economic actors with enough power to upset the balance of embedded autonomy between the state and the private economy on which the success of developmental states is based in the first place. Our insight is similar: state capitalist systems may produce economic actors who may turn their economic power into political power, thus potentially undermining the institutional framework necessary to make state capitalism functioning.

As these state-made economic actors become increasingly internationalized and hence actors that affect institutions and politics beyond the borders of their home country, understanding the determinants of SOEs' institutional strategies becomes a question for business people, policymakers, and academics around the world. In this Element we provide a comprehensive framework that can help with this important task.

The claim that states are not monolithic actors is, of course, not new. However, most efforts to turn this acknowledgment into theories of state activity stem either from political scientists who focus on power relations and conflicts between and within branches of the state bureaucracy such as ministries, or from sociologists like Pierre Bourdieu who analyze the state as a field with opposite social forces (Bourdieu, 2014). This Element seeks to apply a similar logic of decomposition of the state to its economic activity and its economic agents. To do this, we innovate by drawing on concepts and theories from organization studies that allow us to open not only the black box of state economic activity but the even blacker box of SOEs. Our framework allows us to understand how important actors inside state-owned organizations may or may not have preferences that align with other parts of the state and how this may influence their behaviors and strategic actions.

Moreover, as many observers have already pointed out, the concept of state capitalism encompasses wide-ranging practices and logics, which vary across time and countries (see, for instance, Wright et al., 2022). As mentioned already, our framework suggests that SOEs' capacity and willingness to shape their institutional environment also varies across time and countries – and even within countries. What's more, such institutional work on the part of SOEs may significantly shape the outcomes of state capitalism.

Our conceptualization of SOE agency (as strategically important institutional work) implies, indeed, that SOEs can act either as potential multipliers or as inhibitors of state policy, regardless of its objectives (developmental, welfare, strategic industrial...). This implication is in line with the arguments put forward by studies exploring the social, economic, and environmental impact of SOEs' activities – for instance, how SOEs in the oil and gas sector can further or hinder the transition to green energy (see, for instance, the Eskom and EDF cases analyzed in the previous sections; see also Chandra & Chatterjee, 2022; Jaffe et al., 2023). We hope that the framework developed in this Element will equip researchers and practitioners with tools to better understand the question of how state policies and regulations interact with SOEs' market and nonmarket strategies (especially institutional work) to generate positive social, economic, and environmental outcomes.

References

Adebayo, A., & Ackers, B. (2022). Theorising hybridity in state-owned enterprises (SOEs). *Journal of Management and Governance*, *27*(4): 1249–1275.

Aguilera, R., Duran, P., Heugens, P. P. M. A. R., Sauerwald, S., Turturea, R., & VanEssen, M. (2021). State ownership, political ideology, and firm performance around the world. *Journal of World Business*, *56*(1): 101113.

Aguilera, R., & Jackson, G. (2003). The cross-national diversity of corporate governance: Dimensions and determinants. *Academy of Management Review*, *28*(3): 447–465.

Aharoni, Y. (1981). Managerial discretion in state-owned enterprises. In R. Vernon and Y. Aharoni (eds.), *State-Owned Enterprises in the Western Economies* (pp. 184–193). New York: St. Martin's Press.

Aharoni, Y. (1982). State-owned enterprise: An agent without a principal. In L. Jones (ed.), *Public Enterprise in Developing Countries* (pp. 67–76). Cambridge: Cambridge University Press.

Alami, I. (2023). Ten theses on the new state capitalism and its futures. *Environment and Planning A: Economy and Space*, *55*(3): 764–769.

Alami, I., Babic, M., Dixon, A. D., & Liu, I. T. (2022). Special issue introduction: What is the new state capitalism? *Contemporary Politics*, *28*(3): 245–263.

Alami, I., & Dixon, A. D. (2020). State capitalism(s) redux? Theories, tensions, controversies. *Competition and Change*, *24*(1): 70–94.

Alami, I., & Dixon, A. D. (2024). *The Spectre of State Capitalism*. Oxford: Oxford University Press.

Alonso, J. M., & Andrews, R. (2022). Insider lobbying and government contracts: The moderating role of firm size. *European Management Review*, *19*(3): 462–475.

Amatori, F. (1997). Italy: The tormented rise of organizational capabilities between state and markets. In A. Chandler, F. Amatori, and T. Hikino (eds.), *Big Business and the Wealth of Nations* (pp. 246–276). New York: Cambridge University Press.

Apriliyanti, I. D., Dieleman, M., & Randøy, T. (2024). Multiple-principal demands and CEO compliance in emerging market state-owned enterprises. *Journal of Management Studies*, *61*(6): 2406–2436.

Arndt, S. W., & Kierzkowski, H. (eds.) (2001). *Fragmentation: New Production Patterns in the World Economy*. Oxford: Oxford University Press.

Arreola, F., & Bandeira-de-Mello, R. (2018). The differential effects of minority state ownership types on the internationalization of emerging market multinationals from democratic states. *Management International Review, 58* (5): 845–869.

Ballim, F. (2023). *Apartheid's Leviathan: Electricity and the Power of Technological Ambivalence.* Athens: Ohio University Press.

Bałtowski, M., & Kozarzewski, P. (2016). Formal and real ownership structure of the Polish economy: State-owned versus state-controlled enterprises. *Post-Communist Economies, 28*(3): 405–419.

Barca, F. (1997). *Storia del capitalismo italiano dal dopoguerra a oggi.* Bologna: Il Mulino.

Bass, A. E., & Chakrabarty, S. (2014). Resource security: Competition for global resources, strategic intent, and governments as owners. *Journal of International Business Studies, 45*(8): 961–979.

Battilana, J., & D'Aunno, T. (2009). Institutional work and the paradox of embedded agency. In T. B. Lawrence, R. Suddaby, and B. Leca (eds.), *Institutional Work: Actors and Agency in Institutional Studies of Organization* (pp. 31–58). Cambridge: Cambridge University Press.

Battilana, J., Leca, B., & Boxenbaum, E. (2009). How actors change institutions: Towards a theory of institutional entrepreneurship. *Academy of Management Annals, 3*(1): 65–107.

Bellini, E. (2019). A specter is haunting South Africa, renegotiation of PPAs signed between 2011 and 2012. *PV Magazine*, February 20. https://shorturl.at/lloZl.

Berger, S. (2005). *How We Compete.* New York: Currency/Doubleday.

Bernier, L. (2017). Public enterprises as policy instruments: The importance of public entrepreneurship. *Journal of Economic Policy Reform, 17*(3): 253–266. https://doi.org/10.1080/17487870.2014.909312.

Bernier, L., Florio, M., & Bance, P. (eds.) (2020). *The Routledge Handbook of State-Owned Enterprises.* Abingdon: Routledge.

Bertz, J., Quinn, M., & Burns, J. (2024). Public service management reform: An institutional work and collective framing approach. *Public Management Review, 26*(11): 3151–3175. https://doi.org/10.1080/14719037.2023.2207576.

Betz, T., & Pond, A. (2023). Politically connected owners. *Comparative Political Studies, 56*(4): 561–595.

Bischof-Niemz, T. (2019). Opinion: Are renewable IPPs destroying Eskom? *Engineering News*, September 27. www.engineeringnews.co.za/article/are-renewable-ipps-destroying-eskom-2019-09-27.

Bitektine, A., Haack, P., Bothello, J., & Mair, J. (2020). Inhabited actors: Internalizing institutions through communication and actorhood models. *Journal of Management Studies, 57*(4): 885–897. https://doi.org/10.1111/joms.12560.

Boddewyn, J. (1994). Political resources and markets in international business: Beyond Porter's generic strategies. In A. Rugman and A. Verbeke (eds.), *Research in Global Strategic Management*, vol. 4 (pp. 162–184). Greenwich, CT: JAI Press.

Boies, J. L. (1989). Money, business, and the state: Material interests, Fortune 500 corporations, and the size of political action committees. *American Sociological Review, 54*(5): 821–833.

Boisot, M., & Child, J. (1988). The iron law of fiefs: Bureaucratic failure and the problem of governance in the Chinese economic reforms. *Administrative Science Quarterly, 33*(4): 507–527.

Bolino, M. C., & Turnley, W. H. (2003). Going the extra mile: Cultivating and managing employee citizenship behavior. *Academy of Management Executive, 17*(3): 60–71.

Bonardi, J. P. (2011). Corporate political resources and the resource-based view of the firm. *Strategic Organization*, 9(3): 247–255.

Borath, H., Buthelezi, M., Chipkin, I., Duma, S., Mondi, L., Peter, C., Qobo, M., Swilling, M., & Friedenstein, H. (2017). *Betrayal of the Promise: How South Africa Is Being Stolen*. Stellenbosch: State Capacity Research Project. https://pari.org.za/wp-content/uploads/2017/05/Betrayal-of-the-Promise-25052017.pdf.

Bourdieu, P. (2014). *On the State: Lectures at the Collège de France, 1989–1992*. Cambridge: Polity Press.

Bremmer, I. (2008). The return of state capitalism. *Survival: Global Politics and Strategy, 50*(3): 55–64.

Brooks, S. (1987). The mixed ownership corporation as an instrument of public policy. *Comparative Politics, 19*(2): 173–191.

Butzbach, O. (2022). The elusive nature of shareholders' claims over the corporation, or the strange non-death of shareholder primacy. In R. E. Meyer, S. Leixnering, and J. Veldman (eds.), *The Corporation: Rethinking the Iconic Form of Business Organization* (pp. 31–55). Leeds: Emerald.

Butzbach, O., Fuller, D. B., Schnyder, G., & Svystunova, L. (2022). State-owned enterprises as institutional actors: A hybrid historical institutionalist and institutional work framework. *Management and Organization Review, 18*(6), 1032–1076.

Carney, M., Dieleman, M., & Taussig, M. (2016). How are institutional capabilities transferred across borders? *Journal of World Business, 51*(6): 882–894.

Carr, J. H., & Anacker, K. B. (2014). The past and current politics of housing finance and the future of Fannie Mae, Freddie Mac, and homeownership in the United States. *Banking and Financial Services Policy Report, 33*(7): 1–10.

Chandra, R., & Chatterjee, E. (2022). State capitalism in India. In M. Wright, G. T. Wood, A. Cuervo-Cazurra, P. Sun, I. Okhmatovskiy, and A. Grosman (eds.), *The Oxford Handbook of State Capitalism and the Firm* (pp. 697–718). Oxford: Oxford University Press.

Chari, A., & Henry, P. (2004). *Is the Invisible Hand Discerning or Indiscriminate? Investment and Stock Prices in the Aftermath of Capital Account Liberalizations.* NBER Working Paper No. 10318. Cambridge, MA: National Bureau of Economic Research. https://ssrn.com/abstract=509849.

Choudhury, P., & Khanna, T. (2014). Toward resource independence – Why state-owned entities become multinationals: An empirical study of India's public R&D laboratories. *Journal of International Business Studies*, *45*(8): 943–960.

Christensen, C. M. (1997). *The Innovator's Dilemma: When New Technologies Cause Great Firms to Fail.* Boston, MA: Harvard Enterprises as Institutional Actors in Contemporary Business School Press.

Chu, W. W. (2017). *Origins of Taiwan's Postwar Economic Development [Taiwan Zhanhou Jingji Fazhan de Yuanqi]*. Taipei: Academia Sinica.

Claeys, P., Moreno, R., & Suriñach, J. (2010). Fiscal policy and interest rates: The role of financial and economic integration. In A. Páez, J. Gallo, R. N. Buliung, and S. Dall'erba (eds.), *Progress in Spatial Analysis: Methods and Applications* (pp. 311–336). Berlin: Springer.

Clegg, L. J., Voss, H., & Tardios, J. A. (2018). The autocratic advantage: Internationalization of state-owned multinationals. *Journal of World Business*, *53*(5): 668–681.

Cornelissen, J. P., & Werner, M. D. (2014). Putting framing in perspective: A review of framing and frame analysis across the management and organizational literature. *Academy of Management Annals*, *8*(1): 181–235.

Coutant, H., Ducastel, A., & Viallet-Thévenin, S. (2021). Concilier le profit et l'intérêt général: L'État actionnaire dans les dynamiques historiques du capitalisme. Introduction au dossier "Les figures de l'État actionnaire." *Revue de la Régulation. Capitalisme, Institutions, Pouvoirs, 30* (1): 1–32.

Coutant, H., Finez, J., & Viallet-Thévenin, S. (2020). Sur les chemins de la normalisation: Transformations du contrôle des entreprises publiques en France. *Revue Française de Sociologie*, *61*(3): 341–372.

Creamer, T. (2017). Eskom has over recovered R7.6bn in renewables-related costs since 2014. *Engineering News*, July 7. www.engineeringnews.co.za/article/eskom-has-over-recovered-r76bn-in-renewables-related-costs-since-2014-2017-07-07.

Cuervo-Cazurra, A., Inkpen, A., Musacchio, A., & Ramaswamy, K. (2014). Governments as owners: State-owned multinational companies. *Journal of International Business Studies*, *45*(8): 919–942.

Cui, L., & Jiang, F. (2012). State ownership effect on firms' FDI ownership decisions under institutional pressure: A study of Chinese outward-investing firms. *Journal of International Business Studies*, *43*(3): 264–284.

Cull, R., & Xu, L. C. (2003). Who gets credit? The behavior of bureaucrats and state banks in allocating credit to Chinese state-owned enterprises. *Journal of Development Economics*, *71*(2): 533–559.

Dall'Olio, A. M., Goodwin, T. K., Martinez Licetti, M., Orlowski, J. A. K., Patiño Peña, F. A., Ratsimbazafy, F. R., & Sanchez Navarro, D. (2022). *Using ORBIS to Build a Global Database of Firms with State Participation.* Policy Research Working Paper 10261. Washington, DC: World Bank. https://shorturl.at/MzWIE.

D'Andreta, D., Marabelli, M., Newell, S., Scarbrough, H., & Swan, J. (2016). Dominant cognitive frames and the innovative power of social networks. *Organization Studies*, *37*(3): 293–321.

Davie, K. (2019). King Cole defies his energy plan. *Mail & Guardian*, November 29. https://mg.co.za/article/2019-11-29-00-king-coal-defies-his-energy-plan/.

de Geus, C. J., Ingrams, A., Tummers, L., & Pandey, S. K. (2020). Organizational citizenship behavior in the public sector: A systematic literature review and future research agenda. *Public Administration Review*, *80*(2): 259–270.

DiMaggio, P. J., & Powell, W. W. (1983). The iron cage revisited: Institutional isomorphism and collective rationality in organizational fields. *American Sociological Review*, *48*(2): 147–160.

Dorado, S. (2005). Institutional entrepreneurship, partaking, and convening. *Organization Studies*, *26*(3): 385–414.

Dragomir, V. D., Dumitru, M., & Feleagă, L. (2021). Political interventions in state-owned enterprises: The corporate governance failures of a European airline. *Journal of Accounting and Public Policy*, *40*(5): 106855.

Drope, J. M., & Hansen, W. L. (2006). Does firm size matter? Analyzing business lobbying in the United States. *Business and Politics*, *8*(2): 1–17.

Dudouet, F. X., & Joly, H. (2010). Les dirigeants français du CAC 40: Entre élitisme scolaire et passage par l'État. *Sociologies Pratiques*, *21*(2): 35–47.

Economist (2012). The rise of state capitalism. *The Economist*, January 21. www.economist.com/weeklyedition/2012-01-21.

Edwards, T., Kim, K., Almond, P., Kern, P., Tregaskis, O., & Zhang, L. E. (2024). Forgotten globalizing actors: Towards an understanding of the range of individuals involved in global norm formation in multinational companies. *Journal of International Business Studies, 2024*: 1–27. https://doi.org/ 10.1057/s41267-023-00663-6.

Emirbayer, M., & Mische, A. (1998). What is agency? *American Journal of Sociology, 103*(4): 962–1023.

Estrin, S., & Gregorič, A. (2022). State logic and governance: A taxonomy. In M. Wright, G. T. Wood, A. Cuervo-Cazurra, P Sun, I. Okhmatovskiy, and A. Grosman (eds.), *The Oxford Handbook of State Capitalism and the Firm* (pp. 99–128). Oxford: Clarendon Press.

Evans, J. (2022). "Fundamentalist" Gwede Mantashe sticks to his guns, promises "a lot of coal generation by 2030." *Daily Maverick*, February 1. www .dailymaverick.co.za/article/2022-02-01-fundamentalist-gwede-mantashe-sticks-to-his-guns-promises-a-lot-of-coal-generation-by-2030/.

Evans, J., & Ngcuka, O. (2023). How the ANC's years-long delays on renewables plunged SA into darkness and scuppered plan to end blackouts. *Daily Maverick*, January 28. https://shorturl.at/WtfxW.

Evans, P. B. (1995). *Embedded Autonomy: States and Industrial Transformation*. Princeton, NJ: Princeton University Press.

Fan, J. P., Wong, T. J., & Zhang, T. (2007). Politically connected CEOs, corporate governance, and post-IPO performance of China's newly partially privatized firms. *Journal of Financial Economics, 84*(2): 330–357.

Feix, A., & Wernicke, G. (2023). When is CEO activism conducive to the democratic process? *Journal of Business Ethics, 190*(4): 755–774.

Fernandez, R., Hendrikse, R., & Klinge, T. J. (2023). Where state capitalism meets the transnational capitalist state: The ties between Gazprom and Amsterdam's offshore financial center. *Journal of Economic Policy Reform*, 1–22. https://doi .org/10.1080/17487870.2023.2250503.

Fields, K. (1995). *Enterprise and the State in Korea and Taiwan*. Ithaca, NY: Cornell University Press.

Finchelstein, D. (2017). The role of the state in the internationalization of Latin American firms. *Journal of World Business, 52*(4): 578–590.

Fine, C. H. (1998). *Clockspeed: Winning Industry Control in the Age of Temporary Advantage*. Reading, MA: Perseus Books.

Fine, C. H. (2000). Clockspeed-based strategies for supply chain design. *Production and Operations Management, 9*(3), 213–221.

Florio, M., Ferraris, M., Superiore, I., Boella, M., & Vandone, D. (2018). Motives of mergers and acquisitions by state-owned enterprises: A taxonomy and international evidence. *International Journal of Public Sector Management, 31*(2): 142–166. https://doi.org/10.1108/IJPSM-02-2017-0050.

Fuller, D. B. (2007). Globalization for nation-building: Taiwan's industrial and technology policies for high-technology sectors. *Journal of Interdisciplinary Economics*, *18*(2/3): 203–224.

Fuller, D. B. (2013). Building ladders out of chains: China's hybrid-led technological development in disaggregated value chains. *Journal of Development Studies*, *49*(4): 547–563.

Fuller, D. B. (2016). *Paper Tigers, Hidden Dragons: Firms and the Political Economy of China's Technological Development.* Oxford: Oxford University Press.

Fuller, D. B. (2018). The drift: Industrial policy under Ma Ying-jiu. In A. Beckershoff and G. Schubert (ed.), *Assessing the Presidency of Ma Ying-jiu: Hopeful Beginning, Hopeless End?* (pp. 208–223). Abingdon: Routledge.

Fuller, D. B. (2019). Growth, upgrading and limited catch-up in China's semiconductor industry. In L. Brandt and T. G. Rawski (eds.), *Policy, Regulation, and Innovation in China's Electricity and Telecom Industries* (pp. 262–303). Cambridge: Cambridge University Press.

Fuller, D. B. (2021). The increasing irrelevance of industrial policy in Taiwan, 2016–2020. In G. Schubert and C.-Y. Lee (eds.), *Taiwan during the First Administration of Tsai Ing-wen: Navigating in Stormy Waters* (pp. 128–141). Abingdon: Routledge.

Fuller, D. B., Akinwande, A., & Sodini, C. (2003). Leading, following or cooked goose? Innovation successes and failures in Taiwan's electronics industry. *Industry and Innovation*, *10*(2): 179–196.

Galal, A., & Shirley, M. (1995). *Bureaucrats in Business: The Economics and Politics of Government Ownership.* World Bank Policy Research Report. New York: Oxford University Press.

Gereffi, G., Humphrey, J., & Sturgeon, T. (2005). The governance of global value chains. *Review of International Political Economy*, *12*(1): 78–104.

Gerschenkron, A. (1962). *Economic Backwardness in Historical Perspective: A Book of Essays.* Cambridge, MA: Belknap Press.

Giannetti, R. (2013). Industrial policy and the nationalization of the Italian electricity sector in the post-World War II period. In F. Amatori, R. Millward, and P. A. Toninelli (eds.), *Reappraising State-Owned Enterprise: A Comparison of the UK and Italy*, vol. 21 (pp. 242–262). Abingdon: Routledge.

Gintis, H., Bowles, S., Boyd, R. T., & Fehr, E. (eds.) (2005). *Moral Sentiments and Material Interests: The Foundations of Cooperation in Economic Life.* Cambridge, MA: MIT Press.

Girschik, V. (2020). Shared responsibility for societal problems: The role of internal activists in reframing corporate responsibility. *Business and Society*, *59*(1): 34–66.

Gottschalk, K. (2023). Corruption in South Africa: Former CEO's explosive book exposes how state power utility was destroyed. *The Conversation*, May 24. https://theconversation.com/corruption-in-south-africa-former-ceos-explosive-book-exposes-how-state-power-utility-was-destroyed-206101.

Grindle, M. S. (2010). *Constructing, Deconstructing, and Reconstructing Career Civil Service Systems in Latin America*. HKS Faculty Research Working Paper RWP10-025. Cambridge, MA: John F. Kennedy School of Government, Harvard University Press.

Grosman, A., Musacchio, A., & Schnyder, G. (2024). State ownership and political CSR. Paper presented at the Workshop on Governing for Sustainability: Theorizing Business and Government Interactions, May 24, 2024, Bayes Business School London.

Grosman, A., Schnyder, G., Cuervo-Cazurra, A., Okhmatovskiy, I., & Wood, G. T. (2023). Rethinking state capitalism: A cross-disciplinary perspective on the state's role in the economy. *Annals of Corporate Governance*, *7*(4): 252–328.

Groves, T., Hong, Y., McMillan, J., & Naughton, B. (1995). China's evolving managerial labor market. *Journal of Political Economy*, *103*(4): 873–892.

Grundmann, S., & Möslein, F. (2004). Golden shares – State control in privatised companies: Comparative law, European law and policy aspects. *European Banking and Financial Law Journal (EUREDIA)*, *1*. http://dx.doi.org/10.2139/ssrn.410580.

Guo, Y., Huy, Q. N., & Xiao, Z. (2017). How middle managers manage the political environment to achieve market goals: Insights from China's state-owned enterprises. *Strategic Management Journal*, *38*(3): 676–696.

Hafsi, T., Kiggundu, M. N., & Jorgensen, J. J. (1987). Strategic apex configurations in state-owned enterprises. *Academy of Management Review*, *12*(4): 714–730.

Hahn, T., Preuss, L., Pinkse, J., & Figge, F. (2014). Cognitive frames in corporate sustainability: Managerial sensemaking with paradoxical and business case frames. *Academy of Management Review*, *39*(4): 463–487.

Hall, P. (2010). Historical institutionalism in rationalist and sociological perspective. In J. Mahoney and K. Thelen (eds.), *Explaining Institutional Change: Ambiguity, Agency, and Power* (pp. 204–224). Cambridge: Cambridge University Press.

Hall, P., & Soskice, D. (2001). *Varieties of Capitalism: Institutional Foundations of Comparative Advantage*. Cambridge: Cambridge University Press.

Hambrick, D. C. (2007). Upper echelons theory: An update. *Academy of Management Review*, *32*(2): 334–343.

Hambrick, D. C., & Mason, P. A. (1984). Upper echelons: The organization as a reflection of its top managers. *Academy of Management Review*, *9*(2): 193–206.

Hampel, C. E., Lawrence, T. B., & Tracey, P. (2017). Institutional work: Taking stock and making it matter. In R. Greenwood, C. Oliver, T. B. Lawrence, and R. E. Meyer (eds.), *The SAGE Handbook of Organizational Institutionalism* (pp. 558–590). London: SAGE.

Hanto, J., Schroth, A., Krawielicki, L., Oei, P. Y., & Burton, J. (2022). South Africa's energy transition – Unraveling its political economy. *Energy for Sustainable Development*, *69*: 164–178.

Heap, R. (2018). Eskom finally signs 27 controversial PPAs. Tamarindo, April 9. https://tamarindo.global/articles/eskom-finally-signs-27-controversial-ppas/.

Heath, J., & Norman, W. (2004). Stakeholder theory, corporate governance and public management: What can the history of state-run enterprises teach us in the post-Enron era? *Journal of Business Ethics*, *53*(3): 247–265.

Hodgson, G. M. (2006). What are institutions? *Journal of Economic Issues*, *40* (1): 1–25.

Hoffmann, A. (2019). Beware of financial repression: Lessons from history. *Intereconomics – Review of European Economic Policy*, *54*(4): 259–266.

Hofman, P. S., Moon, J., & Wu, B. (2017). Corporate social responsibility under authoritarian capitalism: Dynamics and prospects of state-led and society-driven CSR. *Business and Society*, *56*(5): 651–671.

Holm, P. (1995). The dynamics of institutionalization: Transformation processes in Norwegian fisheries. *Administrative Science Quarterly*, *40*(3): 398–422.

Horton, S. (2006). The public service ethos in the British civil service: An historical institutional analysis. *Public Policy and Administration*, *21*(1): 32–48.

Hsueh, L. M., Hsu, C. K., & Perkins, D. H. (eds.) (2001). *Industrialization and the State: The Changing Role of Government in Taiwan's Economy, 1945–1998*. Cambridge, MA: Harvard Institute for International Development.

Hsueh, R. (2016). State capitalism, Chinese-style: Strategic value of sectors, sectoral characteristics, and globalization. *Governance*, *29*(1): 85–102.

Huang, Y. (2003). *Selling China*. Cambridge, MA: Harvard University Press.

Huang, Y. (2008). *Capitalism with Chinese Characteristics*. New York: Cambridge University Press.

Ibrahim, M., & Aslinda, A. (2013). Relationship between organizational commitment and organizational citizenship behavior (OCB) at government owned corporation companies. *Journal of Public Administration and Governance*, *3* (3): 35–42.

Ingrams, A. (2020). Organizational citizenship behavior in the public and private sectors: A multilevel test of public service motivation and traditional antecedents. *Review of Public Personnel Administration*, *40* (2): 222–244.

Inoué, C. (2020). Election cycles and organizations: How politics shapes the performance of state-owned enterprises over time. *Administrative Science Quarterly, 65*(3): 677–709.

Jackson, G., & Deeg, R. (2008). Comparing capitalisms: Understanding institutional diversity and its implications for international business. *Journal of International Business Studies, 39*(4): 540–561.

Jaffe, A. M., Myslikova, Z., Qi, Q., Zhang, F., Oh, S., & Elass, J. (2023). Green innovation of state-owned oil and gas enterprises in BRICS countries: A review of performance. *Climate Policy, 23*(9), 1167–1181.

Jensen, M. C., & Meckling, W. H. (1976). Theory of the firm: Managerial behavior, agency costs and ownership structure. *Journal of Financial Economics, 3*(4): 305–360.

Jing, R., & McDermott, E. P. (2013). Transformation of state-owned enterprises in China: A strategic action model. *Management and Organization Review, 9* (1): 53–86.

Johnson, S., & Mitton, T. (2003). Cronyism and capital controls: Evidence from Malaysia. *Journal of Financial Economics, 67*(2): 351–382.

Johnstone, P., Rogge, K. S., Kivimaa, P., Fratini, C. F., & Primmer, E. (2021). Exploring the re-emergence of industrial policy: Perceptions regarding low-carbon energy transitions in Germany, the United Kingdom and Denmark. *Energy Research and Social Science, 74*: 101889. https://doi.org/10.1016/j.erss.2020.101889.

Kalasin, K., Cuervo-Cazurra, A., & Ramamurti, R. (2020). State ownership and international expansion: The S-curve relationship. *Global Strategy Journal, 10*(2): 386–418.

Kim, K., & Sumner, A. (2021). Bringing state-owned entities back into the industrial policy debate: The case of Indonesia. *Structural Change and Economic Dynamics, 59*(C): 496–509.

Kornai, J., Maskin, E., & Roland, G. (2003). Understanding the soft budget constraint. *Journal of Economic Literature, 41*(4): 1095–1136.

Kurlantzick, J. (2016). *State Capitalism: How the Return of Statism Is Transforming the World.* New York: Oxford University Press.

Langlois, R. N. (2003). The vanishing hand: The changing dynamics of industrial capitalism. *Industrial and Corporate Change, 12*(2): 351–385.

Lardy, N. R. (2014). *Markets over Mao: The Rise of Private Business in China.* Washington, DC: Peterson Institute for International Economics.

Lardy, N. R. (2019). *The State Strikes Back: The End of Economic Reform in China?* Washington, DC: Peterson Institute for International Economics.

Lawrence, T. B., & Suddaby, R. (2006). Institutions and institutional work. In S. R. Clegg, C. Hardy, T. B. Lawrence, and W. R. Nord (eds.), *The SAGE Handbook of Organization Studies*, 2nd ed. (pp. 215–254). London: SAGE.

Lawrence, T. B., Suddaby, R., & Leca, B. (eds.) (2009). *Institutional Work: Actors and Agency in Institutional Studies of Organizations*. Cambridge: Cambridge University Press.

Lawrence, T., Suddaby, R., & Leca, B. (2011). Institutional work: Refocusing institutional studies of organization. *Journal of Management Inquiry, 20*(1): 52–58.

Lawton, T., Rajwani, T., & Doh, J. (2013). The antecedents of political capabilities: A study of ownership, cross-border activity and organization at legacy airlines in a deregulatory context. *International Business Review, 22*(1): 228–242.

Lazzarini, S. G., Mesquita, L. F., Monteiro, F., & Musacchio, A. (2021). Leviathan as an inventor: An extended agency model of state-owned versus private firm invention in emerging and developed economies. *Journal of International Business Studies, 52*(4): 560–594.

Lazzarini, S. G., & Musacchio, A. (2018). State ownership reinvented? Explaining performance differences between state-owned and private firms. *Corporate Governance: An International Review, 26*(4): 255–272.

Le Monde with AFP (2022). The state is calling on EDF to "limit the rise in electricity prices" in France. *Le Monde*, January 13. www.lemonde.fr/energies/article/2022/01/13/l-etat-met-a-contribution-edf-pour-limiter-la-hausse-des-prix-de-l-electricite-en-2022_6109388_1653054.html.

Lester, R. H., Hillman, A., Zardkoohi, A., & Cannella Jr., A. A. (2008). Former government officials as outside directors: The role of human and social capital. *Academy of Management Journal, 51*(5): 999–1013.

Lethbridge, J. (2020). The politics of state-owned enterprises: The case of the rail sector. In L. Bernier, M. Florio, and P. Bance (eds.), *The Routledge Handbook of State-Owned Enterprises* (pp. 301–321). Abingdon: Routledge.

Leutert, W. (2018). Firm control: Governing the state-owned economy under Xi Jinping. *China Perspectives, 1–2*: 27–36.

Leutert, W., & Vortherms, S. A. (2021). Personnel power: Governing state-owned enterprises. *Business and Politics, 23*(3): 419–437.

Li, H., & Zhang, Y. (2007). The role of managers' political networking and functional experience in new venture performance: Evidence from China's transition economy. *Strategic Management Journal, 28*(8): 791–804.

Liang, H., Ren, B., & Sun, S. L. (2015). An anatomy of state control in the globalization of state-owned enterprises. *Journal of International Business Studies, 46*(2): 223–240.

Lin, L. W., & Milhaupt, C. J. (2013). We are the (national) champions: Understanding the mechanisms of state capitalism in China. *Stanford Law Review, 65*(4): 697–760.

Lincoln, T. (2013). *Reality Check: The Forgotten Lessons of Deregulation and Unsung Successes of Sensible Safeguards.* Washington, DC: Public Citizen.

Liu, Y., Zhang, C., & Jing, R. (2016). Coping with multiple institutional logics: Temporal process of institutional work during the emergence of the one foundation in China. *Management and Organization Review, 12*(2): 387–416.

Loriaux, M. (1999). The French developmental state as myth and moral ambition. In M. Woo-Cumings (ed.), *The Developmental State* (pp. 235–275). Ithaca, NY: Cornell University Press.

Loriaux, M. M., Woo-Cumings, M., Calder, K. E., Maxfield, S., & Pérez, S. (eds.) (1997). *Capital Ungoverned: Liberalizing Finance in Interventionist States.* Ithaca, NY: Cornell University Press.

Maculan, A.-M. (2013). Embraer and the growth of the Brazilian aircraft industry. *International Journal of Technology and Globalisation, 7*(1/2): 41–59.

Mahoney, J., & Thelen, K. (2010). A theory of gradual institutional change. In J. Mahoney and K. Thelen (eds.), *Explaining Institutional Change: Ambiguity, Agency, and Power* (pp. 1–37). Cambridge: Cambridge University Press.

Malingre, V. (2023). Energy crisis: France and Germany at odds over nuclear power market reform. *Le Monde*, July 30. www.lemonde.fr/en/economy/article/2023/07/30/energy-crisis-france-and-germany-at-odds-over-nuclear-power-market-reform_6072149_19.html.

Marin, J. (2020). "It's not a few opponents of Macron who decide the fate of Engie": Behind the scenes of Isabelle Kocher's sudden fall. *Le Tribune*, February 6. www.latribune.fr/entreprises-finance/industrie/energie-environnement/ce-ne-sont-pas-quelques-opposants-a-macron-qui-decident-du-sort-d-engie-dans-les-coulisses-de-la-chute-precipitee-d-isabelle-kocher-838870.html.

Mariotti, S., & Marzano, R. (2019). Varieties of capitalism and the internationalization of state-owned enterprises. *Journal of International Business Studies, 50*(5): 669–691. https://doi.org/10.1057/s41267-018-00208-2.

Mariotti, S., & Marzano, R. (2020). Relational ownership, institutional context, and internationalization of state-owned enterprises: When and how are multinational co-owners a plus? *Global Strategy Journal, 10*(4): 779–812. https://doi.org/10.1002/gsj.1379.

Markus, S. (2008). Corporate governance as political insurance: Firm-level institutional creation in emerging markets and beyond. *Socio-Economic Review, 6*(1): 69–98.

Markus, S. (2012). Secure property as a bottom-up process: Firms, stake-holders, and predators in weak states. *World Politics, 64*(2): 242–277.

Marquis, C., & Qian, C. (2013). Corporate social responsibility reporting in China: Symbol or substance? *Organization Science, 25*(1): 127–148.

McDermott, G. A. (2004). Institutional change and firm creation in East-Central Europe: An embedded politics approach. *Comparative Political Studies, 37* (2): 188–217.

McDermott, G. A. (2007). Politics and the evolution of inter-firm networks: A post-communist lesson. *Organization Studies, 28*(6): 885–908.

McGaughey, S. L., Kumaraswamy, A., & Liesch, P. W. (2016). Institutions, entrepreneurship and co-evolution in international business. *Journal of World Business, 6*(51): 871–881.

McGregor, J. (2012). *No Ancient Wisdom, No Followers: The Challenges of Chinese Authoritarian Capitalism*. Westport, CT: Easton Studio Press.

McKinnon, R. I. (1973). *Money and Capital in Economic Development*. Washington, DC: Brookings Institution.

McMahon, D. (2018). *China's Great Wall of Debt: Shadow Banks, Ghost Cities, Massive Loans, and the End of the Chinese Miracle*. Boston, MA: Houghton Mifflin Harcourt.

Mellahi, K., Frynas, J. G., Sun, P., & Siegel, D. (2016). A review of the nonmarket strategy literature: Toward a multi-theoretical integration. *Journal of Management, 42*(1): 143–173.

Micelotta, E. R., & Washington, M. (2013). Institutions and maintenance: The repair work of Italian professions. *Organization Studies, 34*(8): 1137–1170.

Minzner, C. (2018). *End of an Era: How China's Authoritarian Revival Is Undermining Its Rise*. Oxford: Oxford University Press.

Mizruchi, M. S. (1992). *The Structure of Corporate Political Action: Interfirm Relations and Their Consequences*. Cambridge, MA: Harvard University Press.

Moss, D. A., Bolton, C., & Kimberly, K. (2009). Fannie Mae: Public or private? *Harvard Business School Case 709–025*, February 2009 (revised February 2022). www.hbs.edu/faculty/Pages/item.aspx?num=36928.

Musacchio, A., & Lazzarini, S. G. (2012). *Leviathan in Business: Varieties of State Capitalism and Their Implications for Economic Performance*. Harvard Business School Working Paper 12-108. www.hbs.edu/ris/Publication% 20Files/12-108.pdf.

Musacchio, A., & Lazzarini, S. G. (2014). *Reinventing State Capitalism: Leviathan in Business, Brazil and Beyond*. Cambridge, MA: Harvard University Press.

Musacchio, A., Lazzarini, S. G., & Aguilera, R. V. (2015). New varieties of state capitalism: Strategic and governance implications. *Academy of Management Perspectives, 29*(1): 115–131.

Musacchio, A., & Pineda Ayerbe, E. I. (2018). *Fixing State-Owned Enterprises: New Policy Solutions to Old Problems*. New York: Inter-American Development Bank.

Newman, A., & Zysman, J. (2006). Transforming politics in the digital era. In A. Zysman and A. Newman (eds.), *How Revolutionary Was the Digital Revolution?* (pp. 391–414). Stanford, CA: Stanford University Press.

Ngcuka, O. (2022). Gwede Mantashe has harsh words for Eskom as additional 1,759MW of renewables signed up. *Daily Maverick*, December 8. www.dailymaverick.co.za/article/2022-12-08-mantashe-slams-eskom-as-1759mw-of-renewables-signed-up/.

Noble, G. W. (1998). *Collective Action in East Asia: How Ruling Parties Shape Industrial Policy*. Ithaca, NY: Cornell University Press.

Nolan, P. (2001). *China and the Global Business Revolution*. Basingstoke: Palgrave.

Nölke, A., Ten Brink, T., May, C., & Claar, S. (2019). *State-Permeated Capitalism in Large Emerging Economies*. Abingdon: Routledge.

Nude, W. (2010). *Industrial Policy: Old and New Issues*. UNU-WIDER Working Paper 2010/106. Helsinki: United Nations University-World Institute for Development Economics Research.

O'Connor, D. (2000). Financial sector reform in China and Vietnam: A comparative perspective. *Comparative Economic Studies, 42*(4): 45–66.

O'Hara, G. (2013). Attempts to "modernize": Nationalization and the nationalized industries in postwar Britain. In F. Amatori, R. Millward, and P. A. Toninelli (eds.), *Reappraising State-Owned Enterprise: A Comparison of the UK and Italy*, vol. 21 (pp. 50–67). Abingdon: Routledge.

Okhmatovskiy, I. (2010). Performance implications of ties to the government and SOEs: A political embeddedness perspective. *Journal of Management Studies, 47*(6): 1020–1047.

Oliver, C., & Holzinger, I. (2008). The effectiveness of strategic political management: A dynamic capabilities framework. *Academy of Management Review, 33*(2): 496–520.

Organ, D. W. (1988). *Organisational Citizenship Behaviour: The Good Soldier Syndrome*. Lexington, KY: Lexington Books.

Organisation for Economic Co-operation and Development (OECD) (2015). *OECD Guidelines on Corporate Governance of State-Owned Enterprises*. Paris: OECD.

Organisation for Economic Co-operation and Development (OECD) (2020). *Organising the State Ownership Function: Implementing the OECD Guidelines on Corporate Governance of State-Owned Enterprises.* Paris: OECD.

Organisation for Economic Co-operation and Development (OECD) (2021). *Ownership and Governance of State-Owned Enterprises. A Compendium of National Practices.* Paris: OECD.

Pandey, J., & Varkkey, B. (2020). Impact of religion-based caste system on the dynamics of Indian trade unions: Evidence from two state-owned organizations in North India. *Business and Society, 59*(5): 995–1034.

Park, Y. C., & Patrick, H. (eds.) (2013). *How Finance Is Shaping the Economies of China, Japan, and Korea.* New York: Columbia University Press.

Patrick, H. T., & Park, Y.-C. (1994). *Financial Development in Japan, Korea, and Taiwan.* New York: Oxford University Press.

Peng, M. W. (2003). Institutional transitions and strategic choices. *Academy of Management Review, 28*(2): 275–296.

Peng, M. W., Bruton, G. D., Stan, C. V., & Huang, Y. (2016). Theories of the (state-owned) firm. *Asia Pacific Journal of Management, 33*(2): 293–317.

Pettis, M. (2013). *Great Rebalancing: Trade, Conflict, and Perilous Road Ahead for the World Economy.* Princeton, NJ: Princeton University Press.

Pierson, P. (2004). *Politics in Time: History, Institutions, and Social Analysis.* Princeton, NJ: Princeton University Press.

Piore, M., & Sabel, C. F. (1984). *The Second Industrial Divide.* New York: Basic Books.

Porter, M. (2008). The five competitive forces that shape strategy. *Harvard Business Review, 86*(1): 78–93, 137.

Raynard, M., Lu, F., & Jing, R. (2020). Reinventing the state-owned enterprise? Negotiating change during profound environmental upheaval. *Academy of Management Journal, 63*(4): 1300–1335.

Rayner, J., Lawton, A., & Williams, H. M. (2012). Organizational citizenship behavior and the public service ethos: Whither the organization? *Journal of Business Ethics, 106*(2): 117–130.

Reinhart, C. (2012). *The Return of Financial Repression.* CEPR Discussion Paper 8947. London: Centre for Economic Policy Research.

Reuters (2024). Orlen CEO dismissed as new Polish government seeks change. Reuters, February 1. www.reuters.com/business/energy/orlen-ceo-expects-axe-new-polish-government-eyes-change-2024-02-01/.

Rodrigues, S. B., & Dieleman, M. (2018). The internationalization paradox: Untangling dependence in multinational state hybrids. *Journal of World Business, 53*(1): 39–51.

Rodríguez Bolívar, M. P., Garde Sánchez, R., & López Hernández, A. M. (2015). Managers as drivers of CSR in state-owned enterprises. *Journal of Environmental Planning and Management, 58*(5), 777–801.

Roubini, N., & Sala-i-Martin, X. (1995). A growth model of inflation, tax evasion, and financial repression. *Journal of Monetary Economics, 35*(2): 275–301.

Rudy, B. C., Miller, S. R., & Wang, D. (2016). Revisiting FDI strategies and the flow of firm-specific advantages: A focus on state-owned enterprises. *Global Strategy Journal, 6*(1): 69–78.

Rueschemeyer, D., Evans, P. B., & Skocpol, T. (eds.) (1985). *Bringing the State Back In*. Cambridge: Cambridge University Press.

Ryggvik, H. (2015). A short history of the Norwegian oil industry: From protected national champions to internationally competitive multinationals. *Business History Review, 89*(1): 3–41.

Salamon, L. M., & Siegfried, J. J. (1977). Economic power and political influence: The impact of industry structure on public policy. *American Political Science Review, 71*(3): 1026–1043.

Schmitz, H. (2007). Reducing complexity in the industrial policy debate. *Development Policy Review, 25*(4): 417–428.

Schneider, B. R. (1992). *Politics within the State: Elite Bureaucrats and Industrial Policy in Authoritarian Brazil*. Pittsburgh, PA: University of Pittsburgh Press.

Schnyder, G., & Sallai, D. (2020). Between a rock and a hard place: Internal- and external institutional fit of MNE subsidiary political strategy in contexts of institutional upheaval. *Journal of International Management, 26*(2): 100736. https://doi.org/10.1016/j.intman.2020.100736.

Scott, W. R. (1995). *Institutions and Organizations: Foundations for Organizational Science*. London: SAGE.

Seo, M. G., & Creed, W. D. (2002). Institutional contradictions, praxis, and institutional change: A dialectical perspective. *Academy of Management Review, 27*(2): 222–247.

Shaw, E. (1973). *Financial Deepening in Economic Development*. New York: Oxford University Press.

Shirley, M., & Walsh, P. (2000). *Public versus Private Ownership: The Current State of the Debate*. Policy Research Working Paper 2420. Washington, DC: World Bank.

Shleifer, A., & Vishny, R. W. (1998). *The Grabbing Hand: Government Pathologies and Their Cures*. Cambridge, MA: Harvard University Press.

Situ, H., Tilt, C. A., & Seet, P. S. (2020). The influence of the government on corporate environmental reporting in China: An authoritarian capitalism perspective. *Business and Society, 59*(8): 1589–1629.

Smets, M., & Jarzabkowski, P. (2013). Reconstructing institutional complexity in practice: A relational model of institutional work and complexity. *Human Relations*, *66*(10): 1279–1309.

Smith, C. A., Organ, D. W., & Near, J. P. (1983). Organizational citizenship behavior: Its nature and antecedents. *Journal of Applied Psychology*, *68*(4): 653–663.

Sperber, N. (2019). The many lives of state capitalism: From classical Marxism to free-market advocacy. *History of the Human Sciences*, *32*(3), 100–124.

Stark, D., & Bruszt, L. (2001). One way or multiple paths: For a comparative sociology of East European capitalism. *American Journal of Sociology*, *106* (4): 1129–1137.

Stark, D., & Vedres, B. (2012). Political holes in the economy: The business network of partisan firms in Hungary. *American Sociological Review*, *77*(5): 700–722.

Steil, B., Victor, D. G., & Nelson, R. N. (2002). *Technological Innovation and Economic Performance*. Princeton, NJ: Princeton University Press.

Streeck, W., & Thelen, K. (2005). *Beyond Continuity: Institutional Change in Advanced Political Economies*. Oxford: Oxford University Press.

Sun, P., Mellahi, K., & Thun, E. (2010). The dynamic value of MNE political embeddedness: The case of the Chinese automobile industry. *Journal of International Business Studies*, *41*(7): 1161–1182.

Swanson, D. L. (2008). Top managers as drivers for corporate social responsibility. In A. Crane, A. McWilliams, D. Matten, J. Moon, and D. Siegel (eds.), *The Oxford Handbook on Corporate Social Responsibility* (pp. 227–245). Oxford: Oxford University Press.

Szarzec, K., Totleben, B., & Piątek, D. (2022). How do politicians capture a state? Evidence from state-owned enterprises. *East European Politics and Societies*, *36*(1): 141–172.

Teng, D., Fuller, D. B., & Li, C. (2018). Institutional change and corporate governance diversity in China's SOEs. *Asia Pacific Business Review*, *24*(3): 273–293.

Thatcher, M. (2014). From old to new industrial policy via economic regulation. *Rivista della Regolazione dei Mercati*, *2*: 6–22.

Thelen, K. (2004). *How Institutions Evolve: The Political Economy of Skills in Germany, Britain, the United States, and Japan*. Cambridge: Cambridge University Press.

Thelen, K. (2014). *Varieties of Liberalization and the New Politics of Social Solidarity*. New York: Cambridge University Press.

Thompson, H. (2009). The political origins of the financial crisis: The domestic and international politics of Fannie Mae and Freddie Mac. *Political Quarterly, 80*(1): 17–24.

Thornton, P. H., Ocasio, W., & Lounsbury, M. (2012). *The Institutional Logics Perspective: A New Approach to Culture, Structure, and Process.* Oxford: Oxford University Press.

Thun, E. (2004). Industrial policy, Chinese-style: FDI, regulation, and dreams of national champions in the auto sector. *Journal of East Asian Studies, 4*(3): 453–489.

Thun, E. (2007). The globalization of production. In J. Ravenhill (ed.), *Global Political Economy*, 2nd ed. (pp. 346–371). Oxford: Oxford University Press.

Thurber, M., & Istad, B. (2011). Norway's evolving champion: Statoil and the politics of state enterprise. In D. Victor, D. Hults, and M. Thurber (eds.), *Oil and Governance: State-Owned Enterprises and the World Energy Supply* (pp. 599–654). Cambridge: Cambridge University Press.

Thynne, I. (2011). Ownership as an instrument of policy and understanding in the public sphere: Trends and research agenda. *Policy Studies, 32*(3): 183–197. https://doi.org/10.1080/01442872.2011.561685.

Tihanyi, L., Aguilera, R. V., Heugens, P., Van Essen, M., Sauerwald, S., Duran, P., & Turturea, R. (2019). State ownership and political connections. *Journal of Management, 45*(6): 2293–2321.

Toninelli, P. A., & Toninelli, P. M. (eds.) (2000). *The Rise and Fall of State-Owned Enterprise in the Western World*, vol. 1. Cambridge: Cambridge University Press.

Tonurist, P., & Karo, E. (2016). State owned enterprises as instruments of innovation policy. *Annals of Public and Cooperative Economics, 87*(4), 623–648. https://doi.org/10.1111/apce.12126.

Tooze, A. (2006). *The Wages of Destruction: The Making and Breaking of the Nazi Economy.* London: Penguin.

Tsanova, T. (2017). Investigation starts into Eskom's refusal to sign green PPAs. *Renewables Now*, May 11. https://renewablesnow.com/news/investigation-starts-into-eskoms-refusal-to-sign-green-ppas-568213/.

Useem, M. (1982). Classwide rationality in the politics of managers and directors of large corporations in the United States and Great Britain. *Administrative Science Quarterly, 27*(2): 199–226.

Utterback, J. M., & Suarez, F. F. (1993). Innovation, competition, and industry structure. *Research Policy, 22*(1): 1–21.

Van der Wal, Z., De Graaf, G., & Lasthuizen, K. (2008). What's valued most? Similarities and differences between the organizational values of the public and private sector. *Public Administration, 86*(2): 465–482.

Vernon, R. (1984). Linking managers with ministers: Dilemmas of the state owned enterprise. *Journal of Policy Analysis and Management, 4*(1): 39–55.

Vining, A. R., Laurin, C., & Weimer, D. (2015). The longer-run performance effects of agencification: Theory and evidence from Québec agencies. *Journal of Public Policy, 35*(2): 193–222. https://doi.org/10.1017/S0143814X14000245.

Vogel, S. K. (1996). *Freer Markets, More Rules: Regulatory Reform in Advanced Industrial Countries.* Ithaca, NY: Cornell University Press.

Voinea, C. L., & van Kranenburg, H. (2018). Feeling the squeeze: Nonmarket institutional pressures and firm nonmarket strategies. *Management International Review, 58*(5): 705–741.

Walter, C. E., & Howie, F. J. (2011). *Red Capitalism: The Fragile Foundation of China's Extraordinary Rise.* Singapore: John Wiley & Sons.

Wang, L., Zeng, T., & Li, C. (2022). Behavior decision of top management team and enterprise green technology innovation. *Journal of Cleaner Production, 367*(3): 133120. https://doi.org/10.1016/j.jclepro.2022.133120.

Warwick, K. (2013). *Beyond Industrial Policy: Emerging Issues and New Trends.* OECD Science, Technology and Industry Policy Paper 2. Paris: OECD.

Weinstein, A. (2024). Fannie's CEO contemplates a future after government conservatorship. Bloomberg, January 19. www.bloomberg.com/news/articles/2024-01-19/fannie-mae-ceo-discusses-government-conservatorship-of-gse.

Wiggins, R., Henken, B., Kulam, A., Thompson, D., & Metrick, A. (2021). The rescue of Fannie Mae and Freddie Mac – Module Z: Overview. *Journal of Financial Crises, 3*(1): 447–503. https://ssrn.com/abstract=3903658.

Williamson, O. E. (1963). Managerial discretion and business behavior. *American Economic Review, 53*(5): 1032–1057.

Windolf, P. (2002). *Corporate Networks in Europe and the United States.* Oxford: Oxford University Press.

Wood, G. T., Onali, E., Grosman, A., & Haider, Z. A. (2023). A very British state capitalism: Variegation, political connections and bailouts during the COVID-19 crisis. *Environment and Planning A: Economy and Space, 55*(3): 673–696.

World Bank (2014). *Corporate Governance of State-Owned Enterprises: A Toolkit.* Washington, DC: World Bank.

World Bank (2023). *The Business of the State.* Washington, DC: World Bank.

Wright, M., Wood, G., Musacchio, A., Okhmatovskiy, I., Grosman, A., & Doh, J. P. (2021). State capitalism in international context: Varieties and variations. *Journal of World Business, 56*(2): 101160. http://dx.doi.org/10.2139/ssrn.3799531.

Wright, M., Wood, G. T., Cuervo-Cazurra, A., Sun, P., Okhmatovskiy, I., & Grosman, A. (2022). State capitalism and the firm: An overview. In M. Wright, G. T. Wood, A. Cuervo-Cazurra, P. Sun, I. Okhmatovskiy, and A. Grosman (eds.), *The Oxford Handbook of State Capitalism and the Firm* (pp. 3–24). Oxford: Oxford University Press.

Xin, K. K., & Pearce, J. L. (1996). Guanxi: Connections as substitutes for formal institutional support. *Academy of Management Journal, 39*(6): 1641–1658.

Yan, Z. J., Zhu, J. C., Fan, D., & Kalfadellis, P. (2018). An institutional work view toward the internationalization of emerging market firms. *Journal of World Business, 53*(5): 682–694.

Yaneva, M. (2016). SAWEA files complaint against Eskom. Renewables Now, October 21. https://renewablesnow.com/news/sawea-files-complaint-against-eskom-544003.

Yeung, H. (2016). *Strategic Coupling: East Asian Industrial Transformation in the New Global Economy.* Ithaca, NY: Cornell University Press.

Zara, A., & Delacour, H. (2020). On the fluidity of institutional change: Complex interrelations between multiple types of institutional work during the Serbian transition. *Journal of Management Inquiry, 30*(4): 421–437.

Zhang, K., Pan, Z., Janardhanan, M., & Patel, I. (2023). Relationship analysis between greenwashing and environmental performance. *Environment, Development and Sustainability, 25*(8): 7927–7957. https://doi.org/10.1007/s10668-022-02381-9.

Zhang, X. (2022). Manual override for deposit rates. *Gavekal Dragonomics,* September 22. https://research.gavekal.com/article/manual-override-for-deposit-rates/.

Zietsma, C., & Lawrence, T. B. (2010). Institutional work in the transformation of an organizational field: The interplay of boundary work and practice work. *Administrative Science Quarterly, 55*(2): 189–221.

Zysman, J. (1977). *Political Strategies for Industrial Order: State, Market, and Industry in France.* Berkeley: University of California Press.

Cambridge Elements ☰

Reinventing Capitalism

Arie Y. Lewin

Duke University

Arie Y. Lewin is Professor Emeritus of Strategy and International Business at Duke University, Fuqua School of Business. He is an Elected Fellow of the Academy of International Business and a Recipient of the Academy of Management inaugural Joanne Martin Trailblazer Award. Previously, he was Editor-in-Chief of *Management and Organization Review* (2015–2021) and the *Journal of International Business Studies* (2000–2007), founding Editor-in-Chief of Organization Science (1989–2007), and Convener of Organization Science Winter Conference (1990–2012). His research centers on studies of organizations' adaptation as co-evolutionary systems, the emergence of new organizational forms, and adaptive capabilities of innovating and imitating organizations. His current research focuses on de-globalization and decoupling, the Fourth Industrial Revolution, and the renewal of capitalism.

Till Talaulicar

University of Erfurt

Till Talaulicar holds the Chair of Organization and Management at the University of Erfurt where he is also the Dean of the Faculty of Economics, Law and Social Sciences. His main research expertise is in the areas of corporate governance and the responsibilities of the corporate sector in modern societies. Professor Talaulicar is Editor-in-Chief of *Corporate Governance: An International Review*, Senior Editor of Management and Organization Review and serves on the Editorial Board of Organization Science. Moreover, he has been Founding Member and Chairperson of the Board of the International Corporate Governance Society (2014–2020).

About the Series

This series seeks to feature explorations about the crisis of legitimacy facing capitalism today, including the increasing income and wealth gap, the decline of the middle class, threats to employment due to globalization and digitalization, undermined trust in institutions, discrimination against minorities, global poverty and pollution. Being grounded in a business and management perspective, the series incorporates contributions from multiple disciplines on the causes of the current crisis and potential solutions to renew capitalism.

Panmure House is the final and only remaining home of Adam Smith, Scottish philosopher and 'Father of modern economics.' Smith occupied the House between 1778 and 1790, during which time he completed the final editions of his master works: The Theory of Moral Sentiments and The Wealth of Nations. Other great luminaries and thinkers of the Scottish Enlightenment visited Smith regularly at the House across this period. Their mission is to provide a world-class twenty-first-century centre for social and economic debate and research, convening in the name of Adam Smith to effect positive change and forge global, future-focussed networks.

ADAM SMITH
PANMURE
HOUSE

Cambridge Elements ≡

Reinventing Capitalism

Elements in the Series

Taming Corporate Power in the 21st Century
Gerald F. Davis

*The New Enlightenment: Reshaping Capitalism and the Global Order
in the 21st Century*
Edited by Arie Y. Lewin, Greg Linden, and David J. Teece

Reinventing Capitalism in the Digital Age
Stephen Denning

*From Financialisation to Innovation in UK Big Pharma: AstraZeneca
and GlaxoSmithKline*
Öner Tulum, Antonio Andreoni, and William Lazonick

*Comparing Capitalisms for an Unknown Future: Societal Processes and
Transformative Capacity*
Gordon Redding

*The Future of Work in Diverse Economic Systems: The Varieties of
Capitalism Perspective*
Daniel Friel

*Transforming our Critical Systems: How Can We Achieve the Systemic Change
the World Needs?*
Gerardus van der Zanden and Rozanne Henzen

Aberrant Capitalism: The Decay and Revival of Customer Capitalism
Hunter Hastings and Stephen Denning

*Private Equity and the Demise of the Local: The Loss of Community Economic Power
and Autonomy*
Maryann Feldman and Martin Kenney

*The Transformation of Boeing from Technological Leadership to Financial
Engineering and Decline*
Charles McMillan

*The Fading Light of Democratic Capitalism: How Pervasive Cronyism and
Restricted Suffrage Are Destroying Democratic Capitalism as a National Ideal . . .
And What To Do About It*
Malcolm S. Salter

*State-Owned Enterprises as Institutional Actors in Contemporary Capitalism
and Beyond*
Olivier Butzbach, Douglas B. Fuller, Gerhard Schnyder and Luda Svystunova

A full series listing is available at: www.cambridge.org/RECA